Ivan Ciric has taken us on a remarkable journey of the career of one of the world's greatest brain surgeons, describing his origins in Serbia, training in Europe and the U.S., and how he successfully applied his knowledge and skills to assist innumerable patients during their time of need, teach young surgeons, and inspire many with his dedication and surgical prowess. This is a fascinating account of a fascinating and dedicated physician.

Julian Bailes, MD, Arlene and Marshall Bennett Chairman Department of Neurosurgery and Co-director of the Neurological Institute NorthShore University HealthSystem, Clinical Professor of Neurological Surgery University Of Chicago.

"Listen to the Patient" is a remarkable glimpse into the life, the times, the challenges, and exhilaration of a master neurosurgeon. We were blessed to have Dr. Ciric in the Northwestern family for all of my Chicago years. He was a source of inspiration, reassurance, and serenity when the medical and political worlds seemed to be in chronic chaos. He has captured the essence of the remarkably unique relationship between a patient and a neurosurgeon. As I read his words I am struck by the beneficence of his decision-making and his creativity in the operating theater. His journey should be an inspiration to the next generation of master surgeons.

Hunt Batjer, MD, Professor and Chair of Neurological Surgery, University of Texas, Southwestern. Dr. Batjer is the holder of the Distinguished Lois C.A. and Darwin Smith Chair in Neurological Surgery at UT Southwestern.

Dr. Ciric has delivered a tour de force chronicling a magnificent journey through the extent of his neurosurgical practice and the life surrounding and intertwining with the trials and tribulations of his specialty. It has to be a must-read for any physician in training or in practice and is a very thoughtful, thorough accounting of his experience. Perhaps the greatest take-home message for me is how he describes the lessons learned in wisdom, humility, and humanity by being an honest, ethical physician in an extremely high-risk specialty. When he says "let us treat our patients with the same attributes as we would like our family treated" you can be sure this is the heart and soul of a gifted and caring physician that we can all emulate. Well done, Ivan!!!

Mitchel S. Berger, MD, FACS, FAANS
Berthold and Belle N. Guggenhime Professor
Chairman, Department of Neurological Surgery
Director, Brain Tumor Research Center
University of California, San Francisco

It is no surprise to me that Dr. Ciric, a renowned surgical master, is also a literary master with an intriguing life story. In his book, there is something for everyone: medical history, the every day drama of neurosurgery, and a very personal look inside the mind of a neurosurgeon at the top of his field. In this era of increasingly complex technological innovation and growing bureaucracy, the power of this book lies in the elegance of its simple message: *Listen to the Patient.*

Richard W. Byrne MD
Professor and Chairman,
Department of Neurosurgery Rush University Medical School

Dr. Ciric has written a remarkable book recounting an internal and external journey. It is a journey across physical, emotional, and intellectual time and space. Leaving ones' homeland, no matter how good the destination is a wrenching experience. True, Dr. Ciric early demonstrated superb technical skills. But that is not what made him a great surgeon. The understanding of his own humanity, and the ability to translate that into empathy for his patients...that is what has made him a great surgeon and physician. His book will not tell you that...his genuine modesty would not permit it. But as you follow his journey you will discover his compassion and humility and understand how these enhance and perhaps overshadow mere technical genius.

Jon Grand, Manager
The Book Stall
Winnetka, Illinois

When Dr. Ivan Ciric asked me to read the manuscript of his freshly written memoir titled *Listen to the Patient: Of Life and Neurosurgery*, we had never met in person. So he had no idea that I had scrubbed in the operating room in the Army, as a surgical tech, and had witnessed countless craniotomies. So it was with great anticipation that I read his book.

The first time I saw a surgeon crack-open the skull with a nearly 3-inch -square hole and lay back the dura - the tough outermost membrane enveloping the brain and spinal cord – the first thing I saw was the brain, throbbing forcefully and jumping with each heart beat as if it could squeeze its way out of the head. I was in awe watching the powerful movements of this delicate, convoluted structure which signaled right away that it was the most complicated organ in the body.

Yet it is not the brain itself that is so spellbinding but, rather, what it is capable of: thought, reason, judgements, conscious and unconscious mental processes and activities. Ciric takes us inside the operating room and shares with the reader, "the intricate details and the majestic beauty of brain and spinal cord surgeries." His descriptions of the highly technical life and death struggles in the OR are clearly explained leaving the layman with a new understanding of the tragic losses and glorious victories he has faced. I could not put this book down.

Ciric writes in a splendid poetic style that weaves his countless battles - with the unknown obstacles hidden beneath the wicked tumors, twisted blood vessels and other tricky, life threatening challenges – with captivating stories of his family, colleagues, education and development that pushed him to strive for excellence. We follow Ciric 50-years ago, before the invention of the surgical microscope, CAT scans and MRI diagnostic tools. A time when neurosurgeons almost blindly attacked hidden abnormalities – caused by deadly tumors that contorted the anatomical landscape – forcing Ciric to use, not only his training, but make strategic decisions resulting in devastating failure or magnificent triumphs.

When I was two-thirds through this engrossing book, I remember smiling to myself after deciding I would read this memoir a second time over my next vacation – to once again accompany Ciric on this grand journey that I had been lucky enough to accompany him on for this inspirational passage through his life.

Robert H. Jordan, Jr., Ph.D.
Reporter/Anchor WGN TV-Chicago
Founder/CEO Video Family Biographies
Founder/ Alzheimer's Memory Preservation Project

This is an extremely pleasant walk through reminiscences in the life of a true neurosurgical giant. Colleagues and laity will gather much from his life – well-lived and hard-worked – and the sage lessons derived from the collisions of Past and Present, Success and Failure, Hope and Despair, are eloquently described in this story of dedication and devotion from the humble humanity of this remarkable man. I highly recommend the read.

John L. D. Atkinson MD, FACS
Professor of Neurosurgery
Mayo Clinic
Rochester, Minnesota

As a layman I can appreciate Dr. Ciric's medical career only through his peers. But as a poet I watch Dr. Ciric, the writer, at work and think of Lewis Thomas, whose books were written out of science but are read today as literature. In *Listen to the Patient,* his remarkable stories can only come from a life lived as gracefully and seamlessly as they are written. Frost might have been speaking for Ivan Ciric, the surgeon and writer, when he wrote:

> My object in living is to unite
> My avocation and my vocation
> As my two eyes make one in sight.
> Only where love and need are one,
> And the work is play for mortal stakes,
> Is the deed ever really done
> For Heaven and the future's sakes.

John Barr
President (Retired), the Poetry Foundation

This book is an inspiring odyssey. It's elegant prose describes the character and accomplishments of a premier neurosurgeon. His intellect and surgical prowess are responsible for important technical and conceptual advances in the challenging field of neurological surgery. This is a chronicle of a true "surgeon's surgeon", a valued educator, and a role model for many of his peers.

Edward R. Laws, MD, FACS
Professor of Neurosurgery, Harvard Medical School

LISTEN TO THE PATIENT
Of Life and Neurosurgery

IVAN CIRIC, MD

ARCHWAY
PUBLISHING

Archway Publishing books may be ordered through booksellers or by contacting:

Archway Publishing
1663 Liberty Drive
Bloomington, IN 47403
www.archwaypublishing.com
1 (888) 242-5904

ISBN: 978-1-4808-3122-3 (sc)
ISBN: 978-1-4808-3123-0 (hc)
ISBN: 978-1-4808-3121-6 (e)

Library of Congress Control Number: 2016910877

Print information available on the last page.

Archway Publishing rev. date: 7/21/2016

To my grandsons, Hudson James and Emil Luca

CONTENTS

FOREWORD

Dr. Ciric, in his memoir, *Listen to the Patient,* weaves his personal history into an account of his life's demanding profession, neurosurgery. In it, he relates tales of his privileged aristocratic youth, when he was doted upon by a loving mother and a stern father, and then tells of having to come to grips with the real world when he encounters his own generation outside of his protective family environment. He describes his admiration for his father, whose storytelling he admires, a skill he has clearly inherited. His ability to portray his travels through life within the historical setting is a spellbinding read. He tells the story of his family's travails during the Nazi era, when his father was imprisoned in a concentration camp while he was still a boy and then the family losing all their possessions during the subsequent communist era. He poignantly relates the tragedy of losing a sister from depression.

After finishing his medical degree in Germany, he finally arrives in America, to begin his neurosurgical residency. He generously credits his mentors who helped him along the demanding path to becoming a neurosurgeon. This personal memoir is also generously laced with patient stories and provides an excellent source of the many maladies that a neurosurgeon treats. Ciric' s qualities as a neurosurgeon, husband, and father come through loud and clear, showing us that compassion, commitment, honesty, unrelenting pursuit of excellence, and unwavering professionalism mark his character. Patients and friends alike have benefitted from his care and friendship. This book is a great read, I recommend it with enthusiasm.

Robert F. Spetzler, MD
Chairman, Department of Neurological Surgery
Barrow Neurological Institute
Phoenix, Arizona
February 2016

ACKNOWLEDGMENTS

My gratitude goes to my editor, Mr. George Rumsey, who was on the receiving end of innumerable "final" drafts, for his patience and rigorous editing. My sincere thanks also go to Mr. William Curry, Ms. Adriane Pontecorvo and Ms. Gwen Ash, Archway publishers, for guiding me through the novel experience of being the author of a book. I deeply appreciate the invaluable advice I received from Mr. Jon Grand, Mrs. Marjorie Benton, Mrs. Roberta Rubin, Dr. Corey Franklin, Mr. Scott Clamp and Mrs. Andrea Kott. Last but not least, I am indebted to my wife, Anne, for putting up with my preoccupation while writing these memoirs and for her much-sought-after advice and recommendations.

PROLOGUE

On a time-worn, windswept hill
Where flowers and rainbow are one,
Generations of good and generous people
Have come to rest in eternity.
Eternity as in the ageless river flow
And the rustling of poplar trees in the waning summer breeze.
Eternity as in the morning sunshine rays
Caressing the chiseled stones into a sea of diamonds.
Alas, sorrow and sadness have descended on this serene place,
For the nest in the valley, where my ancestors loved and
cherished,
Is empty and cold and full of dust, weeds and guilt,
Utter desolation triumphant!
And then a miracle at last.
The souls on the hill are rejoicing in glory,
For there is new life in a new nest,
Truly, a loving God's redeeming story!

IVAN CIRIC, MD

INTRODUCTION

The founder of modern neurosurgery, Dr. Harvey Cushing, once said that "the controlling subconsciousness of one's upbringing is something from which time and distance can never wholly wean us." Surely, our past leaves a permanent mark on who we are and how we conduct our lives. And so, after many twists and turns, perhaps the time comes to reflect on the milestones past. To recollect one's past is not easy, for memories fade with the passage of time. Memories also kindle ever-new colorations surrounding an impressionable event that thus grows or diminishes in stature. In *Remembrance of Things Past, Swann's Way,* Proust warns "it is a labor in vain to attempt to recapture our own past, for all the efforts of our intellect must prove futile." With keen awareness of Proust's admonition, I shall nevertheless forge ahead, making sure that my story does not decay into a self-congratulatory Horatio Alger saga or (just as inappropriate) become a self-deprecating elegiac tale, although the reader will probably accuse me of both. In my defense, I shall attempt the impossible task of being unbiased as I weave together the story of my life with the meaning, secrets, and ethical aspects of neurosurgery, including the unique privilege and daunting responsibility of navigating through the hidden nooks and crannies of the human brain. Through a series of select patients' stories and operations, I describe the cascading steps leading up to a neurosurgical procedure for a variety of brain and spinal cord maladies, and I share with the reader the intricate details and majestic beauty of brain and spinal cord surgeries.

For the sake of privacy, patient names were replaced with randomly chosen initials, and I modified the circumstances of encounters. For the same reason, the specific date and location of a given operation were also altered. Any resemblance, therefore, regarding a patient or an operation is a mere coincidence. The patient stories and descriptions of specific surgeries are based exclusively on my memory. No patient records were accessed or utilized for any portion of the book.

OF EXHILARATION AND DESPAIR

Like most neurosurgeons, I have experienced thrill and exhilaration when my healing efforts succeeded and despair when they failed. I intend to tell about both. Before I reminisce on the journey of my life, which brought me from a continent and an ocean away to this promised land, let me begin with the stories of two of my patients, whom I shall call K and J.

A colleague of mine first evaluated K after she began complaining of severe headaches and occasional morning vomiting. As an astute clinician, my colleague immediately recognized the significance of these potentially threatening symptoms as being consistent with increased intracranial pressure. He examined the patient and obtained a magnetic resonance imaging (MRI) test, which revealed the presence of a benign brain tumor, or meningioma, the size of an apple. It was situated within the markedly enlarged left-brain cavity (also known as the lateral ventricle), where it had obstructed the normal flow of brain fluid within a segment of that cavity. The sheer size of the tumor and the unrelenting increase in pressure due to the dammed-up brain fluid were threatening to cause a sudden shift of the brain within the skull, an ominous occurrence that can result in unconsciousness and irreparable brain damage. The only way to prevent such a devastating event was to remove the tumor.

My colleague felt uncomfortable proceeding with the surgery and asked me if I would be willing to intervene in his stead. I agreed and arranged for a meeting with the patient and her husband, a prominent attorney. K was a sophisticated lady—forty-five years old, elegant, and utterly gracious. After showing them the impressive MRI with the large, mottled white blob of a tumor standing out amid the shades of gray of the surrounding brain anatomy, I explained the reason surgery was necessary and the basic steps of the operation. I further explained the general risks of a brain tumor operation, such as an intraoperative hemorrhage, stroke, postoperative seizures, wound-healing problems, and the like.

In K's case, the stakes were even higher because of the location of her tumor in the dominant left cerebral hemisphere. Specific risks relating to the location of K's tumor included loss of new memory acquisition, which would occur if an important nearby memory circuit (known as the fornix) were injured; furthermore, she could sustain a loss of comprehension, which is a difficult-to-rehabilitate type of aphasia, and a loss of peripheral vision.

In essence, I provided the patient with the necessary information as required in the spirit of an informed consent. Besides affording some degree of medicolegal protection to the neurosurgeon, an informed consent is first and foremost a necessary set of information that must be conveyed to the patient and family truthfully, cogently, and always compassionately so as to make it possible for the patient to arrive at a considered decision regarding the proposed surgery.

IVAN CIRIC, MD

The preferred surgical strategy in an operation that requires transit through the brain substance is to choose the safest and preferably shortest corridor through the brain. Another proven tenet is to first convert a large tumor into a smaller one before it is completely removed—not unlike disassembling a schooner before it is removed from the bottle. Finally, it is also prudent to detach the point of tumor insertion into the brain, the root of the tumor, only after the tumor is sufficiently reduced in size. An attempt to rashly detach the root while it is still hidden behind a large tumor can result in uncontrollable hemorrhage with the possibility of a lethal outcome.

On the morning of surgery, in the holding area, I held K's hand for a while before I said a few soothing and encouraging words with a tincture of levity to put her at ease. After I had marked the site of the operation with a wax pencil, K laughed, and as she was wheeled away toward the operating room, she turned around and said in jest, "Doc, let's go for it, and be sure to do the operation on the correct side." As a lawyer's wife, she might have been aware of the harrowing stories of operations performed on the wrong side.

With K anesthetized, we positioned her on her right side, taking care to protect the bundle of nerves in her armpit (known as the brachial plexus) from exposure to pressure during a lengthy operation. The surgical strategy, based on the findings of a functional MRI, was to approach the tumor above the left ear, where it was closest to the brain surface and farthest from the sensory speech area and the memory circuits.

Using an MRI-based intracranial navigation technology, the tumor and the surrounding brain anatomy were mapped out on the patient's head in order to center the incision line and the craniotomy directly over the tumor. The craniotomy in the shape of a manhole cover proceeded along the well-established routine, although with sufficient vigilance to prevent prematurely breeching the dura sheet that covers the brain, which would result in the possibility of a brain injury.

Due to the raised intracranial pressure, the grayish dura sheet covering the brain was under extreme tension, and the usually visible underlying brain pulsations were accordingly absent. To open the dura under these circumstances would have been prohibitive, as the extreme pressure inside the brain would have caused the temporal lobe to be forced out of the skull and become strangulated by the sharp, bony margins of the craniotomy opening, with disastrous consequences. We had several means of lowering the intracranial pressure at our disposal before opening the dura sheet and exposing the brain, all of which were employed. Unfortunately, none of these measures accomplished the task. It was not until the patient's head was elevated some forty-five degrees relative to the heart (by manipulating the operating table) that we noticed a welcome slackening of the dura and a return of brain pulsations. I still remember my sigh of relief!

With the room lights dimmed; the operating microscope brilliantly illuminating the operative field; and the quiet, calm, and comfortable feeling I always experienced when working under the microscope, I safely opened the dura. I paid special attention to keeping a crucial vein on the surface of the temporal lobe out of harm's way, since an injury to that vein more often than not results in a disabling stroke. To my right, also seated, was the neurosurgery resident, who was able to view the operation through a side arm on the microscope. With the dura opened, we could see that the exposed brain was markedly swollen. Resorting again to the intracranial navigation, we determined the desired point of entry through the brain. Fine-tipped electrocautery forceps and microscissors were used to open the shallow groove between the middle and the lowermost temporal hillock (also known as gyrus) for about two centimeters. Beneath the cerebral cortex, we came upon the swollen white matter, which we separated along the path to the tumor as indicated by the navigation probe. Soon, at the exactly predicted depth of just over a half inch, we came upon the thinned-out, translucent wall of the brain cavity, which was opened to expose the dark red to purple tumor mass within it. In keeping with the principle of making a large tumor smaller, we cored out the tumor using ultrasound-based equipment that breaks the tumor mass into the smallest of particles and aspirates them at the same time. In doing so, the tumor capsule began to collapse and recede from the glistening wall of the brain cavity, allowing us to see around the tumor and eventually identify the root of the tumor. The root was imbedded in a finely granular-appearing structure at the base of the brain cavity (known as the choroid plexus), perilously close to the main memory circuit. The root of the tumor was then divided, allowing us finally to get rid of the entire tumor. The process of tumor removal took about three hours—seemingly forever—mostly because each time the ultrasound probe was used to break up and aspirate the tumor interior, there was bleeding from the raw tumor surface, with the blood welling up within the resulting tumor cavity. We could not allow the accumulated blood to spill outside the tumor cavity and into the brain cavity, as it would have quickly spread throughout the series of brain cavities, forming a clot well beyond the area of the surgical exposure, from which it could not be retrieved. Such a calamitous event is potentially lethal due to the pressure exerted by the blood clot on the vital centers for cardiac and respiratory functions in the brain stem. Consequently, the progress of the operation was slowed by the need to frequently control the points of bleeding from the raw surface inside the tumor.

With the tumor removed, we paused briefly to admire the sublime majesty of the exposed anatomy: here the unscathed memory circuit and there the basal ganglia, the central-to-the-brain knolls made up of neurons that regulate the fluidity and smoothness of our movements and play a role in how we perceive our environment. Deeper yet is the limbic system, the seat of our emotions that color, for better or worse, our daily desires, passions, anger, and joy. With all these structures pulsing synchronously with the heartbeat, they were continuously washed clean under the small waves of clear brain fluid whose circulation had been restored by the removal of the tumor.

Satisfied that there were no residual points of bleeding, we embarked on the closure by meticulously paying attention to each and every step in the process, such as stitching together the dura, replacing and anchoring the skull flap, and closing the scalp, as each of these steps has its own pitfalls.

In the recovery room, the patient woke up bright-eyed and bushy-tailed with no neurologic deficits. As I went out to the family room, my body language must have immediately revealed that I was the bearer of good news. To be able to convey such good news to the loved ones after a challenging brain operation is one of the most satisfying experiences in the life of a neurosurgeon. Following her discharge from the hospital,

IVAN CIRIC, MD

K continued to do well. She was followed for a number of years by our neuro-oncology team with no recurrence.

Unfortunately, the multitude of the salutary outcomes in the life of a neurosurgeon is offset by a few stories of failures that leave a permanent mark of despair on the neurosurgeon's soul. Poor outcomes are predominantly the result of a complex or insurmountable nature of a neurologic illness. Unfortunate outcomes also tend to occur more frequently early in the professional life of a neurosurgeon, when the clinical acumen lacks in sagacity and the surgical alacrity is short on experience. Still, unfavorable outcomes are rarely the consequence of straightforward technical inaptitude of the neurosurgeon. Instead, they are more likely to be the postscript of a nuanced lack of wisdom or judgment, such as failing to recognize correctly the nature or severity of a neurologic illness and making wrong decisions relative to the surgical indications, timing of the operation, and choice of the surgical strategy.

This brings me to the story of J, who came under my care shortly after I began practicing in 1967. I happened to be in the operating room, working on releasing the median nerve in a young seamstress suffering from carpal tunnel syndrome, when the circulating nurse said, "Dr. Ciric, the emergency room just called; they have admitted a patient with severe headaches." After talking to the emergency room (ER) physician on the phone, I learned that J, forty-six years old, had developed severe headaches two days prior to admission to the ER and that he had vomited on the morning of admission. On examination, he was listless and lethargic, albeit able to communicate and fully oriented. I was told that his neurologic examination revealed no focal abnormalities, save for stiffness in his neck. I assumed that the patient had a ruptured cerebral aneurysm, although I also considered the possibility of meningitis. Since this patient was seen long before CT scan technology became available, which today would have established the correct diagnosis within ten minutes from arrival to the emergency room, I asked the resident to go to the ER and perform a spinal puncture in search for blood or infection in the cerebrospinal fluid. As the spinal puncture was being done, the patient suddenly cried out and became unresponsive, his respirations ceased, and the vital signs began to fail, necessitating intubation, assisted respirations, and cardiac support. An emergent cerebral angiogram at this point revealed the presence of an acute obstructive hydrocephalus.

What is an obstructive hydrocephalus? Inside the right and left hemispheres of the brain are symmetrical horseshoe-shaped cavities, the lateral ventricles. As I mentioned in K's case, at the bottom of the lateral ventricles lies the choroid plexus. The function of the choroid plexus is to continuously produce brain fluid (also known as the cerebrospinal fluid), to the tune of close to a pint a day. The brain fluid flows from the lateral ventricles through a narrow opening into a slender cavity positioned in the midline, known as the third ventricle. From the third ventricle, via a series of connected channels and cavities contained in the brain stem, the brain fluid flows out of the brain. Any obstruction to the free flow of brain fluid through these cavities will cause it to accumulate under an ever-increasing pressure upstream from the point of blockage, a disturbing event that can lead in a relatively short time to irreversible neurologic complications, including the loss of consciousness. The obstruction in J's case was caused by a benign cyst, which was sitting like a boulder in the third ventricle, blocking the brain fluid from leaving the lateral ventricles. Consequently, the brain fluid began to accumulate in the lateral ventricles under high pressure, which is in fact the obstructive hydrocephalus.

But what caused J to become suddenly unconscious and stop breathing during the lumbar puncture? Well, as the lumbar puncture released some of the cerebrospinal fluid from the spinal canal, the severely increased intracranial pressure caused the brain, including the brain stem, to shift and become impacted in the opening of the skull where it joins with the spine. This can result in a sudden loss of consciousness and failing vital signs.

Having completed the operation on the carpal tunnel, I ran downstairs to the ER only to be confronted by the disastrous neurological scene of an unconscious man on life support. In the meantime, in order to lower the intracranial pressure, the resident had also performed a procedure known by its acronym as an EVD (external ventricular drainage), whereby the dammed-up brain fluid is detoured externally into a series of sterile containers. Because of the patient's young age and the benign nature of the cyst, in spite of the poor prognosis, I thought we ought to give him a chance for at least some recovery by removing the cyst.

As I stepped out to the waiting area, I met a tall, elegant, and composed, though understandably anxious, woman, whose pleading eyes and outstretched arms as she stood up to greet me were asking for good news and hope. Avoiding eye contact, with slumped shoulders and trembling voice, I must have conveyed the opposite with my body language—desolation and hopelessness. I explained the dire situation at hand and my recommendation to proceed with craniotomy to remove the cyst.

Bewildered, aggrieved, and in a state of disbelieving shock, the wife consented. The cyst was removed via a small right frontal craniotomy with no difficulties, yet it was too late to reverse the course. J passed away a few days later without ever coming off life support.

As I gained wisdom and experience over the years and with the advent of contemporary noninvasive diagnostic tools, the deleterious outcomes, while still as aggrieving and remorseful as the first one, have become rare occurrences between successful operative results. The introductions of the CT scan in the 1970s and, even more so, MRI technology in the 1980s were the most important milestones in the evolution of noninvasive diagnostic tools that have contributed to a quantum leap in the accuracy and timeliness of the neurologic diagnosis. The CT scan is a digitally reconstructed three-dimensional X-ray image, while the MRI utilizes the magnetic field that swirls around each of us to generate images of brain and spine anatomy, pathology, and even function with incredible clarity and resolution. On the surgical technology side, the introduction of the operating microscope in the mid-1960s was the single most important technical innovation in my professional life. The operating microscope made it possible to convert brain operations previously performed in a deep and poorly lit space, visualized with only one eye due to limited exposures, into binocular, 3-D procedures in a brilliantly illuminated and magnified operative field.

Nevertheless, in spite of the riveting progress in diagnostic tools and surgical technology, neurosurgery is still a very personal human endeavor. Neurosurgeons then and now have been vested with a unique responsibility the moment they have a scalpel in their hands, for the fine line between a life with dignity and the devastation of humanity in their patients can be incredibly thin. The outcome of a neurosurgical procedure is dependent on not only the absolute precision in the execution of a neurosurgical task, but also on deriving beforehand a correct diagnosis and on formulating a sound, anatomically based, and humanly tailored treatment strategy. Neurosurgeons surely remember with exhilarating gratification the patients whose lives they changed for the better. No neurosurgeon ever forgets the woman near death from a ruptured aneurysm who had her life saved and function restored, the patient with a spinal tumor who could walk again, the patient nearly blind due to a pituitary tumor who could see again, the suffering one who became pain free, and many others. At the same time, neuro-surgeons certainly also remember, with utmost humility and a lifelong crestfallen contrition, the occasional patient they have failed and whose life, as a result, might have been extinguished or left for worse.

HERITAGE

The region in the Balkans I hail from has a rich ethnic heritage, a true melting pot if there ever were one. From the ancient Celtic people, followed by the Roman legions who marched through the area on cobblestone roads paved for them by the empire and so durable that some of them are still in use today, to the hordes of Huns who briefly swept through the Balkans under Attila in the fifth century and the Slavic tribes (including my Serbian and Montenegrin people) who settled in the Balkans in the seventh century, all have left not only a DNA footprint but also a token of customs and beliefs and a legacy of culture and religion. It was in the ninth century that missionary brothers Saints Cyril and Methodius brought Christianity to the Slavs. This was also the beginning of the centuries-old discord, as the Croats and Slovenes accepted the Roman Catholic Latin Mass, while the Bulgarians, Greeks, Macedonians, Montenegrins, Romanians, and Serbs received their baptism in the Eastern Orthodox rites. After establishing a thriving state over several centuries in the central and southern parts of the Balkans, culminating with the sprawling empire of Czar Dusan in the early fourteenth century, the Serbs were among the first to challenge the Ottoman

Empire's ambition of a European conquest. Thus, it was in June of 1389 that the Serbian Kingdom confronted the Ottoman Empire under Sultan Murad I at the battle of Kosovo Field. The Serbs were vanquished, and their Prince Lazar was slain. I know of no other nation that celebrates its defeat as a symbol of national pride and perseverance. Even though Serbia ceased to be an independent state in the wake of that faithful battle, the Ottomans did grant a certain degree of autonomy to Prince Lazar's successor, Despot Stefan, albeit in a vassal relationship to the Ottoman Empire. As a diplomat and statesman, Stefan proved to be a veritable match to Murad's successors. Through deft diplomatic relationships with Hungary to the northeast and Venice in the west (during which he frequently changed sides) and by helping the Ottomans defeat the Wallachians at the Battle of Rovine and an alliance of western kingdoms at Nicopolis, Stefan managed to keep the Serbian lands united and prosperous. His successor, a nephew by the name of Djuradj Brankovic, did not have the same leadership qualities, and the Ottomans gradually but surely withdrew their previously granted concessions. The Battle of Kosovo Field opened the doors for the Ottoman Empire to overrun the Balkans and central Europe and advance north as far as Vienna.

The Ottoman Empire held sway over the Balkans for close to five hundred years, with all its human toll and political and cultural repercussions, including the fact that the Balkan nations did not experience the Renaissance. The harshness of the Ottoman occupation is the subject of the 1961 Nobel Prize–winning novel *The Bridge on the Drina* by the Serbian author Ivo Andric. As the Ottoman Empire began to crumble at its fringes half a millennium after the battle at Kosovo, the Serbian people insurrected and established an independent Serbian state in 1804 under the leadership of Djordje Petrovic, known as Karadjordje. His progeny established the Karadjordjevich royal family line, albeit not as Karadjordje's immediate successors, since another Serbian noble family, the Obrenovich clan, claimed the throne for most of the nineteenth century.

The Montenegrin history, my mother's heritage, differs from the Serbian. Being a mountainous country with nearly impassable mountain roads, Montenegro was never conquered by the Ottomans save for occasional forays into the main cities, from where they would soon be expelled by the Montenegrin warriors. The largely peaceful succession of Montenegro's rulers, from the Balsic to the Crnojevic and the Petrovic dynasties, proceeded uninterrupted by outside interference. The Petrovic dynasty established the theocratic form of governance in that a relative of the reigning bishop, usually a nephew of the ruler, would enter the monastic life in order to assume the mantle of leadership. The rulers were usually enlightened and progressive. A Crnojevic ruler established one of the first printing operations in Europe after he brought a replica of Gutenberg's printing machine in the sixteenth century. The most enlightened ruler was Petar Petrovich Njegos, a philosopher, poet, and statesman whose epic poem "The Mountain Wreath" is considered one of the masterpieces of European literature. The Petrovic dynasty ended after World War I, when Montenegro was incorporated into the newly formed Kingdom of Serbs, Croats, and Slovenes under the banner of the Serbian king Peter I Karadjordjevich.

Eager to learn more about my heritage, my wife, Anne, and I set out recently on a pilgrimage through Serbia and Montenegro, visiting a number of Serbian and Montenegrin monasteries that date back to the early eleventh century. We visited the mausoleum of the Karadjordjevich dynasty, which features beautiful mosaics showing the history of Serbia from its inception. From there, we visited several monasteries erected by Serbian rulers prior to the invasion of the Ottomans. The monasteries are in fact shrines where the Serbian kings and queens frequently retreated to a monastic and ascetic life. The monasteries of Kalenic, Ljuboshinje, Zicha, and Studenica are religious enclaves dominated by a Romanesque church with ancient murals depicting the life of the rulers, many of whom were sainted, and religious scenes from the Bible. It was our impression that at all the monasteries, the centerpiece of piety, prayer, and Christian symbolism was veneration of the Mother of Christ.

In the monastery at Cetinje, we were shown three reportedly authentic Christian relics: one of the earliest icons of Mary from the first century, a piece of the cross Jesus was supposedly crucified on, and, most incredulously, the hand of John the Baptist. According to the lore, when crusaders had to abandon Jerusalem and flee from the advancing Ottomans, they first took the relics to the Island of Rhodes in the Aegean Sea, where they remained for several hundred years under the crusaders' watch. As the Ottoman armada threatened once again, the relics were taken by the crusaders to Malta, where they again remained for several hundred years. Shortly before Napoleon conquered Malta, the crusaders received an invitation from Czar Paul of Russia (son of Katherine the Great) to bring the relics to Russia for safekeeping. Czar Paul adorned the container holding the relics with diamonds and precious stones and kept them in the imperial treasury.

Several centuries later, under the flames of the 1917 Communist revolution, Russian nobility and clergy escaped, taking the relics to Berlin. As Hitler ascended to power, the exiled Russian nobility and clergy took the relics to Belgrade. Just before the surrender of the Kingdom of Yugoslavia to Germany, the Serbian patriarch took the relics to Montenegro and hid them in the monastery of Ostrog, perched amazingly on a small clearing high up on the nearly vertical face of a mountain and barely accessible. He himself hid there as well. A traitor revealed the hiding place of the prelate, who was eventually apprehended and sent to the concentration camp in Dachau. The relics remained hidden in the monastery. Eventually, with the fall of Communism and Nazism, the relics were transferred from the monastery of Ostrog to a more accessible monastery in Cetinje, where they can be viewed.

THE ANCESTRAL HOME

As the Ottoman Empire spread its wings over the Balkans, my ancestors fled north and settled in the Danube Valley, along the Austro-Hungarian border. The town I grew up in, with the tongue-twisting name of Sremski Karlovci, dates back to Roman times. Karlovci has ranked prominently in the pages of history since 1699, when it hosted the Congress of Karlovci. In a sepulchral chapel built for the occasion, with separate entrances for each of the negotiating potentates, a peace treaty was hammered out between the victorious Holy League—consisting of Austria-Hungary, Poland, Venice, and Imperial Russia—and the defeated Ottoman Empire. This treaty marked the start of the Ottoman decline and the ascendancy of the Hapsburg monarchy as one of the dominant geopolitical players in Europe. As for my town, it remained within the far-flung monarchy for the ensuing 220 years. After the demise of the Austro-Hungarian Empire in the wake of the Great War and the Treaty of Versailles, of which Serbia was a signatory on the side of the victorious Allies, our province and town were united with the newly created Kingdom of Serbs, Croats, and Slovenes, later renamed Yugoslavia. During the Second World

War, Sremski Karlovci was incorporated into the Independent State of Croatia, a puppet state of Nazi Germany, only to find itself after the war again within the boundaries of a reconstituted Yugoslavia, albeit not a kingdom any longer but instead under the Communist regime of Marshal Tito. Finally, since the unfortunate, violent disintegration of Yugoslavia into its constituent states in the 1990s, our town and the surrounding province of Srem have been in the fold of the Republic of Serbia.

In the 1930s, Sremski Karlovci was a pastoral town of about six thousand souls on the south bank of the Danube, some forty miles north of Belgrade. The townsfolk consisted of an equal number of ethnic Serbs and Croats living peacefully and in harmony with each other. The best view of our town and the surrounding countryside was from the hillside cemetery. Down in the valley, the mighty Danube flowed silently only to disappear in the ever-present haze of the horizon some ten kilometers to the south. The rhythmic clatter of the passing trains along the river, though distant, could be heard at the cemetery seemingly for an eternity. To the northeast, on the other side of the river, the endless plane of the dried-out basin of the ancient Pannonian Sea, with its emerald-green pastures dotted with the gold of the many wheat and cornfields, stretched as far as the eye could see. If one turned around facing west, the eye was met by the rolling hills of the Fruska Gora, speckled with numerous vineyards, their geometric orderliness interrupted here and there by the lushness of verdant meadows and the brilliance of wildflower colors. To the north, just below the cemetery, was the city itself, with its gabled rooftops perched close together, almost one on top of the other. In the center of the city, the Orthodox cathedral's two spires, like two tall sentries, towered above the Byzantine edifice of my high school and the stately neobaroque buildings from the Austro-Hungarian times.

In the town, the main street had asphalt, while the side streets were either cobbled or paved with ancient stones from Roman times. Come spring and late into the fall, shepherds would come down the main street before sunrise to collect the livestock to be taken to the pastures. Separate shepherds blew different-sounding horns for cattle, pigs, and sheep. The farmers would open the doors to their yards and let the animals join the procession. What always amazed me was that upon return from the pastures in the evenings, each animal, except for the sheep, found its way alone and without any guidance to the open doors of its master's home, be it up the hill or down closer to the river. With the livestock off to the pastures, farmers and winegrowers would make their presence known by the metallic thud of the horseshoes and the rattle of the iron-covered buggy wheels thumping against the asphalt of the main street. While newspapers were available at the single kiosk in the town square, the local news and ordinances were brought to the attention of the townsfolk by a uniformed village crier, who would go from one street corner to the next, announcing his presence with a small drum that hung around his neck. He would read the announcements with an air of utmost importance and a self-appropriated sense of authority. Most of the time, the only person listening to his message would be the roaming street vendor with a box slung over his shoulder, displaying his wares: an assortment of small combs, mirrors, hair oils and pomades, ribbons of different colors, and other items.

Besides being known for its Rieslings and Burgundies, Sremski Karlovci was also a place of intellectual pursuits. The oldest Serbian high school was established in our town in 1791, although the origins of higher education date back to 1725, when the Russian empress Catherine I helped establish a Latin gymnasium with the purpose of promoting classic education among the Serbian population. The Austro-Hungarian Empire was relatively benevolent in allowing commerce and promoting economic well-being among its ethnic minorities. On the other hand, the empire did not permit the establishment of a university by a minority group. Those who desired a university degree had to go to Vienna or Budapest. Thus, a number of graduates with advanced degrees who had difficulty obtaining university positions taught at Sremski Karlovci High School. Among prominent Serbian intellectuals who graduated from the high school was romantic nineteenth-century poet Branko Radicevic, who was instrumental in popularizing the newly created Cyrillic phonetic alphabet that replaced the ancient Church Slavonic script. The scholarly reputation of the high school and the fact that Sremski Karlovci had also been the seat of the Serbian Orthodox patriarchate made our town the important center of the Serbian cultural heritage that it remains to this day.

Our house, down in the valley, was surrounded by homes of farmers, beehive keepers, and wine producers, all of whom kept horses and had livestock. When remodeled by my parents in 1936, the original house, which fronted the street, received an addition at a right angle to the front and thus assumed an L-shaped form. The lengthy brick-and-stucco house was fairly typical for homes built in small towns across Austria-Hungary and northern Yugoslavia. The single-story house had heavy oak doors fit for a fortress, leading to a cavernous portal that was cool in the summer and conserved heat in the winter. Over the doors and just under the eaves, reliefs of two heavenly angels guarded the entrance. Next to the entrance, the house had a row of windows with pull-down blinds and folding wooden shutters. Inside the portal, a flight of stone stairs covered with a seriously worn red runner carpet, a remnant from the days of family fortunes, led up into the house. At the top of the stairs, high French doors opened into a lengthy corridor covered with the same runner, appointed with a variety of easy chairs and coffee tables, and framed with paintings. On the east side of the corridor, large windows opened onto the garden with views of the poplar trees along the banks of the Danube in the distance. Double French doors led from the corridor into rooms facing the street to the west: my father's library and parlor rooms, decorated with hand-painted wallpapers of different colors and designs, mostly in purple and blue motifs, and appointed with an eclectic combination of Biedermeier furniture. In my father's library hung a painting of the family patron, St. Nicholas, painted by my uncle. At the end of the corridor, one entered a spacious dining room with a heavy oak dining table surrounded by three elaborate period credenzas. The bedrooms and the guest rooms were in the new addition. All the rooms in the new addition had ceramic wood stoves that could be fired up from the hall by the help, thus obviating the necessity to disturb the occupants of the rooms. Because of the sloping property, the new addition had two stories, with the servants' quarters, kitchen, and utility rooms on the mezzanine and ground floors. The house was my mother's pride and a place where she always returned to find refuge and solace from the vagaries of life during and after World War II and where she stoically braved all the misfortunes that befell the family.

In the back of the house, facing east, our property sloped in a terraced fashion toward a retention pond immediately behind a brick wall that circled and insulated the yard from the pond and the neighbors. In the summer, the pond was a breeding ground for mosquitoes, especially since many households emptied their stable refuse and other discarded material into the pond. Along the wall facing the pond were magnificent common purple, Josee, and white lilac bushes, whose fragrance helped ameliorate the unpleasantness wafting from the pond. The upper tier of the yard had a patio next to the house, where the family would gather for lunch and, in the height of summer, for dinner as well. In front of the patio were two rows of wild roses on either side of a round clearing. In the center of the clearing was a fountain that most of the time stayed dry because of the precarious water supply from the steadily diminishing stream in the artesian well and the irreplaceable attrition of the water pump housed in the basement. From the patio tier, stone steps led down to an English garden with a rectangular bed of royal roses surrounding the lawn. The roses and the lawn were framed by a knee-high hedge of evergreens. A gravel path descended from the portal, along the north side of the garden, toward the lower yard, in which a variety of cherry, plum, and pear trees stood beside ageless chestnut trees and a single evergreen tree. I will always remember the home of my youth with fondness and nostalgia.

FAMILY

As I grew older, I frequently visited the graves of my ancestors at the crest of the cemetery and let my imagination browse at will. There is a broken-in-half small cross made out of a pale pink marble and covered with dull green moss, with a barely readable inscription indicating that the deceased was a seven-year-old boy. It is the grave of my grand-grand-grand uncle, who died, alas, after a stone hurled from a sling, David style, struck him in the temple. Imagine his mother's grief as she buried her only son. Little did she know then that she would be blessed, or cursed, with a long life during which she would also bury her only daughter and granddaughter—my grandmother—in addition to her husband, the grand sire of the family, a man of means and influence. I never understood why he commanded the nickname the Toothy: Jovan "Zuban" Popovich. They are all there in that cemetery, descended through Zuban's daughter. I suppose this is why the graves contain remains with so many different names: Popovich, Krecharevich, and Ciric. It is not surprising that a family friend once suggested that I was born with an antique, rusted, bourgeois silver-plated spoon in my mouth.

My father was born with phocomelia, a rudimentary left hand. His parents died early, his mother when he was seven months old and his father, a prominent lawyer and chief counsel to the Serbian patriarchs in Sremski Karlovci, when he was six years old. My father grew up in the home of his uncle, Milan Ciric, the parish priest of the Serbian Orthodox Cathedral in Novi Sad, the capital of the province of Vojvodina. The good priest and his wife were childless, puritanical, and stern but also endowed with a lot of common sense. In bringing up my father and his two older brothers, they imparted the importance of education and emphasized values such as truth, honor, and respect for everybody regardless of nationality, creed, or station in society, an important message in a multiethnic society of different faiths. In contrast, little emphasis, if any, was placed on acquiring material goods, perhaps in part because of the inherited wealth. The good priest was also a wise steward of the boys' considerable fortunes, mostly land that they inherited from the mother's side of the family, which he administered with responsibility.

The brothers grew up surrounded more by books than by parental love. The insatiable desire to learn fell on the fertile ground of two exceptionally gifted boys: my father, Stevan, and his older brother Ivan. They read philosophy and history, and they mastered calculus. As their hobby, they constructed mathematical equations. They learned foreign languages and became fluent in several. My father also became an expert chess player, eventually attaining the title of a national chess master. I have a photograph of my father playing several games simultaneously without looking at the boards at the Novi Sad Chess Club, winning most of the games. My father studied history and philosophy at the University of Budapest and Vienna. To the best of my knowledge, he did not graduate with a degree. Instead, due to a chronic lung illness for which he sought remedy in Switzerland's mountain resorts, he returned home to Sremski Karlovci and assumed the position of a high school history professor. Photographs of my father when he was a young man show a handsomely chiseled face reminiscent of Greek sculptures, with a thoughtful expression and a touch of Slavic melancholy to his countenance. His deeply set light brown eyes, beaked nose, high forehead, shock of prematurely white hair, and natural proclivity for courteous demeanor made him look not only distinguished and manly but also, above all, void of any pretense and trustworthy and respectful. He was a spell-binding storyteller and orator who captivated his audience not only with his eloquence but also, in great measure, with his clearly conceived message, always backed by a large repository of facts that his gargantuan memory easily retrieved as needed from wherever such facts might be stored in the brains of gifted people. I suppose it was because of his reputation as a man of truth and dignity, his oratory, and his own desire to promote parliamentary rights in response to the ever-greater assertion of power by the Yugoslav king Alexander that my father entered politics and was elected congressman from our district in 1929. Over a period of ten years, until 1939, he served variously as congressman, minister of education, and president (speaker) of the Yugoslav Parliament. The imposing Parliament building in Belgrade was built and inaugurated during my father's tenure as president. In spite of my father's newly gained prominence, my parents elected not to move to the capital city, Belgrade, and instead decided to keep our home in Sremski Karlovci as their residence. My father's political life kept him most of the time in Belgrade and away from home, save on weekends and during vacations, when my parents would take us children along, on occasion even abroad to Nice, Venice, or Karlovy Vary. My father's political career ended in 1939, when he was dismissed as the minister of education. The reason behind my father's dismissal from the government was his opposition to a treaty that allowed Germany free passage through the Kingdom of Yugoslavia in its quest to occupy the coveted oil fields at Ploesti, Romania. I am proud not only of my father's accomplishments but also, even more so, of his uncompromising honesty and ethics as a public servant.

My father's older brother Vladislav, a medical student in Vienna, succumbed to the ravages of tuberculosis. The oldest brother, Ivan, responded to the call of his faith and, after attaining doctorates in Semitic languages from the University of Vienna and in theology from the University of Moscow, returned home and took the vows as a Serbian Orthodox monk, when his name was changed from the secular Ivan to the monastic Irinej. My uncle was consecrated as the bishop of the Novi Sad diocese within a few years. He was fluent in most European languages and could read the original Hebrew, Latin, Greek, and Aramaic texts, which helped him greatly as he pursued his doctoral thesis on the book of the prophet Habakkuk. He also composed church music and became an accomplished painter.

My mother, fifteen years younger than my father, was a high school senior when they first met. They married after a ten-year courtship. She was the daughter of the town's former mayor, who was also a vineyard owner who sold his wines to various establishments locally and in the district. She was the second youngest of seven siblings. The photographs of my mother as a young woman and a painting of her that my father commissioned (by a relative who was a successful society painter, Urosh Predich) show an oval-shaped, perfectly proportioned face with slightly prominent cheeks. Her black hair, parted in the middle, contrasts the pallor of her face, dominated by her slightly slanting hazel eyes, which exude calm and confidence. Her rather thin lips, usually set in a barely perceptible hint of a smile, gave the impression, I think, of utmost determination. She was a petite woman of enormous energies that served her well early on in her marriage as the wife of a prominent political figure and later on in life as a protector of the family during the ravages under Nazi occupation during the Second World War. My maternal grandfather saw to it that my mother's five brothers attained higher education that led to successful careers in law, medicine, banking, and business. His older daughter, Katherine, remained single, and because she did not get a higher education, he willed his house and the vineyards to her. I will always remember my aunt with gratitude for her purposeful influence in my upbringing and for helping me out through medical school when my parents fell on hard times after World War II.

EARLY CHILDHOOD MEMORIES

One of my earliest memories relates to an evening when my parents entertained guests. It was one of those occasions that children view differently from adults. Most of all, I remember the sweet smell of the ice cream—vanilla, cherry, peach, and strawberry—emanating from cylindrical containers stored on the concrete floor of the basement pantry, where the temperatures were cool even in the height of the summer. I also remember the long and sleek chauffeured limousines disgorging elegantly dressed men and women. It must have been quite a sight with all the fancy cars arriving in a cloud of dust on a balmy summer evening, with the townsfolk taking in the spectacle. I suppose the mooing of cows and neighing of horses in the neighbor's yard added to the incongruity of the scene. My mother, always the perfect host, had an uncanny ability to not only keep the evening afloat but also turn it into a success. She engaged her guests in conversation by always being on the offensive with questions about everything and anything and by flirting with flattery. Meanwhile, the family wine would warm up even the toughest skeptics who had accepted this invitation to dinner in the country with ambivalence. As the evening progressed, my father would take over with his stories, for he had a story for each and every occasion, with the guests soaking in every word with rapt attention. During the dinner, my mother presented my sisters and me, dressed in our Sunday best, to the assembled guests. My sisters were taught how to curtsy. I don't know why my mother did this, but she did display me proudly. This adoration, however, was not for what I was—or, better said, for what I was not. It is my impression that my mother saw in me the embodiment of her own dreams of being the mother of a little prince in abstraction. To her, I was unassailable in my supremacy of simply having been born into a prominent family—supremacy that she was convinced gave me the right to be more distinguished, intelligent, and talented than any of my peers. I think she had an idealized image of what aristocrats' children look like: the haircuts of pages or medieval knights, ridiculous pastel-colored knitted shorts buttoned to laced shirts, and patent-leather shoes completing the effete outfit. God forbid my hands should get soiled or my knees get bruised. "Why," she would say indignantly, "this is for the children of ordinary people, who are allowed to participate in such life-threatening situations as running after a ball on the street, or even worse, heavens, only rowdies with no class play this low-life, vulgar sport of soccer."

Truth be said, I was probably not so blatantly obtuse to realize, even as a little boy, that something was amiss, especially since my presumed superiority fizzled when my cousins from Belgrade would come for a visit. They were taller, leaner, and faster than I; were skillful in playing all kinds of ball games; and divinely played accordion and piano. They were genuinely adored by everybody assembled at the dinner table. Even my mother's eyes would sparkle in recognition of Vladan's and Pero's antics and performances. The realization of being an outlier, to say the least, something akin to an adored picture, can leave a lasting effect on a five-year-old child. It took a number of years for different circumstances to purge my self-image of a little porcelain prince, and I assumed a new coat of arms.

My quirky upbringing, which included English and a succession of German governesses, had the advantage of exposing me to foreign languages early in life. For the first five years of my education, I did not attend regular classes at the local public school. Instead, I was homeschooled. This was another of my mother's idiosyncratic notions—that I should not mix with so-called ordinary townsfolk's children, lest I contract a serious illness at worst or adopt unacceptable, rowdy behavior at best. My instructor was my father's godmother, Sophia Knezevic, a teacher by profession, whose house across town I used to go to for private tutoring. She was in her late seventies, was plain looking, and always dressed in gray to match her graying hair, which she combed straight and knotted in a bun at the back of her head. She always smelled of garlic. What stood out in this plainness were her sparkling blue eyes and her commonsense approach to life. She taught me reading, writing, and arithmetic, but she was also a storyteller. Mostly, she told old town stories; she recalled long-forgotten town gossip, including my father's mischief when he was a boy. She immediately spotted that I was being brought up in my mother's fantasy world, which she began to dismantle with great ease and dispatch, cleansing me from my pseudopolished veneer. "After all," she would argue, "your mother is one of us ordinary people. Yes, her father was the town mayor, but he was a down-to-earth merchant and vineyard owner who was always a gentleman and modest to the core."

To my mother's astonishment, her little unassailable prince began to walk with his hands in his pockets; I started playing in the street and even managed to persuade my mother to shed my page haircut. I had a good time with my teacher, Sophia; I felt secure and confident while at her house, with its well-tended rose garden studded with figurines and ceramic garden balls of different bright colors perched on white wooden sticks. The candied fruit she served me along with a cup of warm milk added to the allure of the visit. I must have mastered the grammar school material just sufficiently enough to pass the required exams at the end of each year.

It was at the beginning of a summer recess that I first met my oldest friend, Mike, who came to our house for a visit accompanied by his mother, a teacher in a nearby village. We were both seven years old at the time. I took Mike by his shirtsleeve to the cherry tree in our orchard, where we helped each other reach for the branches weighted with cherries. I suspect my mother initiated this get-together as a way to end my isolation, since she probably realized that social interaction might be, after all, important in the development of a child. Mike and I saw each other frequently, playing imaginary games of hide-and-seek in the bushes of our garden. Mike lived with his paternal grandmother in a house with earthen floors and a thatched roof up the hill from our home. Visiting Mike was an eye-opener, as I got acquainted with living circumstances different from those I grew up in.

THE NEFARIOUSNESS OF THE WAR YEARS

In April of 1941, the Ciric family's life changed abruptly and irrevocably. I had my homework in front of me as I was dreamily watching the dance of dust particles carried by the afternoon sun rays struggling to enter the piano room through the crack in the blinds, when I heard shots fired through the window and into the ceiling. I remember being scared, but I also felt safe when my mother—the wizard of tough situations, a problem solver, and a protector—threw me onto the floor and indicated that I should follow her, crawling on our knees, down to the relative protection of our concrete basement kitchen. This was the day when our town surrendered to the mighty Wehrmacht, albeit not without a fight. I remember the commotion several days before the war broke out; people were coming to see my father, who was by then out of politics and government. It was a few days before the war began that a tall and elegant gentleman wearing a dark suit and holding a homburg under his arm came to visit my father. Dressed in white linen trousers and an old jacket over a crumpled shirt, my father was sitting in his favorite wicker chair in the orchard, reading and enjoying the early wafts of spring with a cup of coffee at his side, sitting on a small, rickety, and (from having braved many winters outdoors) somewhat-rusted table. I happened to be nearby, so I overheard a heated conversation during which the well-dressed visitor seemed to plead with my father to be reasonable, while my father seemed just as adamant in rejecting whatever the visitor was proposing. I recall my father saying, "I did nothing wrong. I am not going anywhere," upon which the visitor bid his adieu and, with his homburg atop his patrician head, turned around and slowly went up the gravel path toward the house and the waiting limousine.

Years later, I learned from my mother that the visitor was an emissary of the newly formed Yugoslav government under the leadership of General Simovic, which was about to leave into exile just a few days ahead of the certain defeat and occupation of the country by Germany. Germany was about to declare war on Yugoslavia in the wake of a popular uprising and a coup by the Yugoslav army, which rebelled against an agreement of cooperation between Nazi Germany and Yugoslavia. Prince Paul, who succeeded King Alexander as a regent after the king's assassination in 1934, and Prime Minister Cvetkovic, who orchestrated this agreement, were forced into exile. Evidently, the new government under General Simovic considered my father a person of trust on whom they could rely in the formation of the government in exile and thus wanted him safely out of the country.

A few days after our town surrendered to the Wehrmacht, the local Nazis, the *Ustasha*, took control of the town and came at dusk to arrest my father. The Ustasha team consisted of the newly appointed town mayor, a burly man with a plethoric face who lived a few houses down the road from us; the police chief, an obsequious coward who kept apologizing for the intrusion ("I am just doing my duty," he would say repeatedly); and two other men my mother did not recognize when she peered through the window to see who was banging on the massive oak doors of our house. One of the men was dressed in the Ustasha uniform, and the other was in a leather trench coat, even though in the setting sun, it was still warm and pleasant. When my mother opened the window and inquired what the mission of their visit was, the police chief replied that they would like my father to come with them to the city hall so they could talk to him. They did not elaborate on what they wanted to talk about. My mother refused to open the door, keeping the delegation at bay, saying that my father did not feel well enough to leave the house. It is still incomprehensible to me that she had the courage to defy four menacing men in a standoff that lasted through the night. The following morning, exhausted from the night's vigil, she relented, and my father was taken away. That was the last time I saw my father for seven years. Upon his return home after the war, weakened and ailing, my father was reluctant to talk about his hideous experiences in the concentration camp, and we respected his unwillingness in this regard.

Upon the surrender of the Kingdom of Yugoslavia to Germany at the beginning of World War II, the Yugoslav northern province of Backa was ceded to Hungary, which clearly sympathized politically with the Axis powers. As the bishop of the Backa diocese and the spiritual leader of a sizable Serbian community at the beginning of the war, my uncle had a fair degree of influence with the political establishment of Hungary. This made it possible for him to shield and rescue more than two thousand women and children from being deported to the

Nazi concentration camps. For this, he was posthumously honored by the Serbian government in the 1990s and more recently by the city of Novi Sad in 2015.

According to my mother, Bishop Irinej also intervened on behalf of his brother, who was thus spared execution. Upon his release, my father found refuge in the Belgrade home of my maternal uncle Dr. George Milich and his family, where he stayed until the end of the war. I believe my father's reluctance to reminisce on the suffering he and his comrades were subjected to during those horrid days in the camp was influenced by his remorse that he'd survived, while his friends had perished to the last man.

In the wake of my father's arrest, all through the war, the intermittent raids by the Ustasha continued, during which they would round up local Serbs who were then sent off to the concentration camps, such as Jadovno and later Jasenovac, most of them never to be heard from again. The raids were more the result of a required quota of detention of Serbs rather than a targeted dismantling of prewar political structure. Why would they have otherwise had the need to arrest and send to the concentration camp four beautiful, innocent teenage sisters who lived a few blocks down the street from us, three of whom perished while in the camp? The raids were in fact so haphazard that if one were lucky to be indisposed and not hear the ominous knock on the door, he or she could escape being hauled to the train station and herded into a cattle car, albeit likely at the misfortune of a neighbor who would be taken away instead.

Because of the raids, my mother decided that it would be safer if the family moved away from our home and huddled at my Aunt Katherine's house about three-quarters of a mile away. I clearly remember the quiet, snowy winter evening in 1943 when my mother, with my sisters and me in tow, set off for my aunt's home. I remember the feeling of joy and hope as we trudged through the hushed stillness of the heavy snowfall, wishing the moment would never end. I liked to gaze into the falling snowflakes reflected in the street lamps as they appeared in the light and trace them until they reached the snow blanketing the earth. I wondered where their journey began, and I admired their freedom from the reality of life in Karlovci. We entered my aunt's house through a rusted front door, using a key the size of a bayonet. The hall had a concrete floor and iron arches supporting the ceiling, as one sees in respectable wine cellars. To the left were creaky, partially rotten, immense wooden doors leading into a deep cellar that for perhaps half a century, if not longer, was never entered since it was continuously under two to three feet of water. Evidently, this infrastructure problem did not bother the otherwise solidly built brick-and-concrete house. I still wonder what was hidden in that dark and sinister dungeon—most likely old wine barrels and paraphernalia used by wine growers of that time. To the right, a partially glassed-in door covered with a lace curtain opened into a tiny landing. To the right of the landing, occupying the ground floor was the long-ago-shuttered great-grandfather's general store. The store was full of old desks, display tables, and scales, all strewn between a maze of broken chairs and tables and covered with dust and cobwebs. Along the walls were rows of shelves and vertically stacked drawers that once contained the merchandise, a true treasure trove for antique hunters. (Decades later, my wife's discerning eye spotted among the crumbling furniture a set of Victorian dining room chairs and a graceful Victorian sofa, which she appropriated and had restored.) From the landing, a polished but also creaky staircase covered by a once-fashionable Viennese runner that had been trampled down by innumerable half-cleaned shoes, many times straight from the muddy vineyards, curved around a statue of Artemis leading up to the dining room. The fire in the ancient white-and-blue ceramic stove was on, and my aunt, some fifty-six years of age at the time, sat in her easy chair next to the stove. Her older brother stood next to the stove, warming his hands against the hot tiles. He had the foremost right to it since it was by his doing that the hearth was kept alive each day. My uncle was quite a character, as only a retired judge can be. Particular with his attire, he always wore spats, even in summer, and he was a stickler for ingrained habits of daily activities. My aunt was short of stature, though agile. She had a round but pleasant face once admired by many suitors, all of whom failed to capture her heart. Her light blue eyes exuded warmth and compassion. She meticulously kept her eyebrows plucked each day, and she wore relatively garish lipstick and rouge that contrasted with her natural pallor, which had been protected from the sun her entire life. Indeed, the skin of her face was that of a maiden. After all, that is what she was. The dining room table was set for dinner. No matter the war and the related shortcomings, the table was covered with a tablecloth that belonged to who-knows-what ancestor, and this was always emphasized. "You know, Ivan, one day this tablecloth will belong to your wife," my aunt would say. I wondered if the numerous stains from the even-more-numerous dinners would also be part of the dowry. Heck, one could not wash such extravagant items as a tablecloth in the winter. That would have to wait for the summer.

The illumination was provided by an oil lamp with a wick that flickered under a green glass shade, contributing to a cozy and peaceful atmosphere. The sumptuous feast consisted of flat corn bread made without yeast, for there was no yeast to be had during the war; bacon; cottage cheese; and onions—great stuff. Drinking water in Karlovci was in abundance. There was always wine for my uncle, the quality of which would depend on the generosity of my aunt's sentiments, which dictated which barrel to raid on a particular day.

My aunt's house was surrounded by two spacious cobbled yards. The property included a stable with usually four to five horses; a shed with two coaches, a yellow one for every day and a lacquered black one for special occasions; and chicken and turkey coops. In the adjoining yard, there was a large dry cellar containing huge aged oak barrels filled with Riesling and Traminer wines, grape presses, and other items necessary to produce wine. As a child, I loved to roam around the yards, peer into the stable, and search for chicken and turkey eggs, which were oftentimes hidden in the hay of the stable mangers.

Throughout the years, I enjoyed going to my aunt's vineyards some four kilometers out of town. The road to the vineyards merged for a short distance with a stretch of the highway before swinging down a ravine along the Danube, becoming a dusty path in the summer and a muddy track when it rained, which it did frequently at the time of grape harvest. After escaping my mother's protective hold, I used to join the day workers in the vineyard when they ate their meager lunch of bread, raw bacon, and onions and sit around with them in the shade of a giant acacia tree, listening to their stories and folk wisdom. Later on, while in high school, I would invite my friends Mike and Luka to come along or join my uncle, the retired judge, to pick cherries in the spring and grapes at harvest time, which we brought home to our families. Ah, there is nothing sweeter than a bushel of ripe grapes plucked directly from the vine. Back home, the grapes were spread out on newspapers in the attic, where they would remain as a source of vitamin C throughout the winter.

A town physician's wife, even though of Serbian origin, was in good standing with the local fascist government. She saved many a life by notifying Serbs in town of an impending Ustasha raid. This made it possible for my mother, my aunt, my two older sisters, and me to leave Karlovci under the cover of darkness through the back alleys and escape by ferry across the Danube to the town of Novi Sad in Hungary. I remember the feeling of dread at seeing in the distance the portly silhouettes of the town mayor and the police chief conspiring under a lamppost and the sense of relief from imminent danger once the ferry began to sail across the Danube.

We found refuge in the residence of my uncle Bishop Irinej. The bishop's palace was a neoclassical edifice of red bricks with a marble facade and a hint of Byzantine overtones, adjacent to the Novi Sad Orthodox cathedral. During my family's stay there, I continued my education under my uncle's auspices. At the end of each day, with his duties for the day finished, I would go to his study, where he taught me history, geography, foreign languages, and math, oftentimes late into the night and with a candle burning next to the open text—electricity was scarce, and blackouts might be declared to shield us from Allied bombing raids. My uncle was a tall, slender, and athletically built man who was balding by the time I knew him, and he had a lengthy but nicely trimmed white beard. He was not without wit and humor and enjoyed hearing a good joke, when his usually serious mien would soften and his eyes would twinkle. He walked as if tiptoeing. Every morning, he would prostrate himself in prayer with a series of pious push-ups. He also found solace in his faith, his church, and his vast library of several thousand books that he had collected over the years.

Meanwhile, my younger sister, Kitty, was staying with my maternal uncle at his apartment in Novi Sad. He was single, dashing, tall, and always elegantly dressed. His previously angelic face (he even once posed for the likeness of the archangel Michael) was deformed by injuries he'd sustained in an explosion at the beginning of the war. Although Uncle Branko did not adopt my sister legally, he treated her as his own child, with unabashed love and tenderness. Trained as a lawyer, he dabbled in land and real estate with reasonable success. He was generous to me, having supported me during my student days by supplying me with clothes and giving me small cash gifts for birthday and Christmas; he was even more generous toward my parents when my father lost all of his possessions in the aftermath of World War II.

Thus, the family shuttled by ferry across the Danube between the Independent State of Croatia and Hungary, as the situation demanded based on the information supplied to my mother by the doctor's wife. During one of the ferry crossings over the Danube, we witnessed a Jewish couple attempting to escape from the Ustasha rule in Croatia. They were refused entry into Hungary and sent back on the same ferry to Croatia. We could see across the river as the border guards struck the couple with their rifle butts and then whisked them into a shack. I will never forget the image of those two kind people, with whom we had struck up a conversation on the ferry ride to Hungary.

THE PERFIDY OF THE POSTWAR YEARS

At the Yalta conference in February of 1945, the Allies agreed that Yugoslavia would be placed under Soviet Russia's sphere of influence. This geopolitical decision gave the Communist underground, the Partisans under the leadership of Marshal Tito, the upper hand in forming the postwar government at the expense of the royal guerillas, the Chetniks, and the royal government in exile. The Chetnik leader, General Draza Mihajlovic, was lured into Tito's orbit under the pretext of negotiations, at which time he was apprehended and summarily executed after a briefly staged kangaroo court, ostensibly for crimes committed against the state. As a prominent leader in the prewar Kingdom of Yugoslavia, my father was also taken to prison by the Communist regime, where he languished for eighteen months without ever being charged.

My father's failing health and our age difference (my father was my senior by close to half a century) inevitably influenced our relationship after he returned home in 1947. I admired my father. I was in awe of him for his accomplishments, and I respected him immensely for what he was as a man. At the same time, I also had a latent fear of him and was always on guard, lest I transgress the limits of what he considered acceptable behavior. To be loud or boastful or to come home late for dinner was bad manners. To show a chink in the parentally bestowed armor of excellence, as when bringing home less-than-stellar high school report cards, was deemed an unacceptable lack of effort. Even playing a chess game to a draw in the local amateur tournament was considered a weakness, for my father preferred the valor of winning and the courage of losing to the mediocrity of a draw. My mother wanted me to have piano lessons, which I did until, after a few lessons, my father asked the piano teacher whether he thought I had musical talent. "Frankly," said the teacher, "I doubt it, but we can give it a try." That was my last lesson. I fully understand my father's decision to cancel my lessons in view of the meager income he earned as a high school student tutor.

Fatherly upbringing also included pronouncements rather than a discourse, as, for example, when he admonished me one day not to covet money and to be frugal. I suspect that in the absence of any intimacy between my father and me, the tacit understanding in the family was that my own life motifs would evolve simply by following the example of my father's virtuous character and societal accomplishments. It is only now, while I am writing these memoirs, that I understand my father's affectionate parental intentions, the best he knew how, for which I will always be infinitely grateful.

Upon my father's release from prison, the Communist regime expropriated all of his possessions except for the family home. The proceedings to that end bore all the characteristics of the early sordid postwar Communist demagoguery with prearranged public hearings. A Communist agitator would shout slogans, such as "Comrades, is it fair for Stevan Ciric to own ten acres of vineyards, a one-hundred-forty-acre farm, and rental houses, when he never sets a foot on these properties and never does any decent manual labor on these properties himself?" This cry for redistribution of wealth was answered with a prearranged chorus of "No!" and "Take it away, and give it to the hardworking people whose hands are covered with blisters from toiling for the rich!" and similar assertions of justice under the newly minted Communist laws. So in less than an hour, my father was stripped of his possessions.

Meanwhile, my uncle Bishop Irinej was also placed under house arrest in Novi Sad by the new Communist regime; he underwent daily interrogation and was beaten for several weeks. Whether the blows to the head he sustained when stones were hurled at him by Communist agitators on a visit to one of the parishes did permanent damage or whether my uncle developed an Alzheimer's-like dementia in the last years of his life is uncertain. As a physician and a neurosurgeon, I tend to favor the latter explanation. The bishop developed severe memory loss that, toward the end, made him unable to recognize even the closest family members. His mentally locked-in state persisted for months before he faded away. I remain indebted to the leadership of the Serbian Orthodox diocese in Novi Sad for caring for my uncle, my surrogate father and mentor, with dignity in the bishop's residence in Novi Sad during the most trying time in his life and for granting him a celebratory entombment in the cathedral crypt, alongside the remains of his ecclesiastical predecessors.

THE DRUDGERY OF HIGH SCHOOL

My high school years are a blur of eight years of asserting myself. The fifth, sixth, and seventh grades were mostly spent in defending myself from bullies and from kids who came from families that found new prominence in the Communist regime. I was much younger than some of the classmates who had missed school due to the war. I remember especially one fellow, Marko, who was at least five years older than I and a true ruffian. He threatened to beat me unless I did his homework for him. I was ridiculed for my upbringing and called a bourgeois fatso from the vanquished upper class. Insulting remarks were also made on the account of my parents, including claims that they should be punished too.

In search for support in the class, I turned to my oldest friend, Mike, who was a classmate of mine through high school. It did not take long for Mike to exert his leadership and become the dominant force in our relationship. The subservient behavior on my part was not only because he offered protection from my harassers but also in large measure because Mike was the class valedictorian all through high school and, as such, assumed the aura of a man with vision and values to be admired and strived for. I will always remember Mike with a deepest sense of esteem and appreciation for his leadership when it was needed.

At home, after school, I would find consolation in books ranging from the exploits of Jules Verne's heroes to Harriet Beecher Stowe's *Uncle Tom's Cabin*, James Fennimore Cooper's *The Leatherstocking Tales*, and Karl May's westerns, all of them my favorites and stoking my imagination. Later on, as I advanced toward the senior years and under the influence of my favorite history professor—a gentle, erudite, and highly myopic maiden—I took up classics from Dickens to Balzac and from Dostoyevsky to the prescribed Soviet-era writers, such as Maxim Gorky. Emulating my history teacher, I kept a record of books I read, which I proudly shared with her.

In high school, I also enjoyed spending time with another friend, Luka, exploring the poplar woods along the Danube riverbanks. Luka came from a family of winegrowers—good, hardworking, and completely unpretentious people. Gradually, we decided it was time to start exploring the opposite riverbank, so we began to swim across the Danube, some days more than once. Looking back, surely this was a foolish thing to do, with undercurrents along the shores and all the ship traffic. Well, somehow we survived. We used to climb on boats that larger ships bound upstream trawled along and then dive back into the water a mile or two upstream so we could leisurely swim back to one or the other shore at exactly the level of our town. On one such foray, Luka and I were nearly doused with tar thrown at us by a Russian mariner. We would often end our day of Danube escapades at his house, having a slab of warm white bread covered with a layer of lard and green onions. In addition, while we were not supposed to do this, most days, we would sneak into the family's wine cellar and have a gulp of Riesling drawn through a wine pipette directly from the barrel.

To experience the Danube in the summer at dusk is quite a thrill, with the sky azure blue, heavy, and warm. This is the time of the day when the Danube appears to be at peace with itself; its mirror-like gray surface is without a ripple, and its stillness is interrupted only by fishermen tapping against the water as they angle for catfish. On one such summer evening, as I was just about to slip into my shorts, ready to go home after a day of sunning, swimming, and other less-than-useful activities, a friend of mine suddenly showed up with the obvious intention of going for a swim. He was two years older than I and a freshman at the prestigious medical school in Zagreb. His academic reputation was legendary. He had spent the whole summer of 1948 studying in Zagreb and had recently come home for a brief holiday. We talked for a while, when he said jokingly, "Well, I'd better be going; it will be dark pretty soon, and pirates tend to roam the Danube at night." We laughed, and off he went, diving headfirst from a tree stump on the riverbank, smoothly and elegantly, almost without a ripple. He never resurfaced. It took me an unforgiving long time to realize that something was seriously wrong before I summoned the few remaining bathers to help me in rescuing my friend. We waded into the river where he'd dived in and where, submerged by the higher-than-usual Danube water level, a wartime German concrete defense bunker stood. We found him barely conscious and with no movements in his arms or legs. I remember George lying on the sand, his slender six-foot body struggling for air, his handsome face hollow, and his dark hair, neatly cut in preparation for his return to Zagreb, full of sand. *My God*, I thought, *why didn't I warn him of the submerged bunker? How could I have been so reckless not to mention it to him?* I wanted so much to reverse time and take away the abysmal last five minutes of my life. It took a bike ride into town by a young man, who was there to enjoy the scenery, to summon an ambulance, which transported my friend to the regional hospital in Novi Sad, some ten kilometers away. My friend passed away that night.

As an upperclassman, I gradually gained acceptance and became friends with two other boys in the class, Mile and Toma, who were considered hip and who dated the most popular girls in the class. Mile was short and had darting eyes set deeply under prominent eyebrows. He held his head high and proud but without conceit. In spite of his stature, classmates looked up to him, and his word was usually final. Toma, of Dalmatian heritage, was tall and athletically built and had a shock of curly blond hair and soft blue eyes that expressed calm and sincerity. He was the goalkeeper on the high school varsity soccer team, and as such, he was adored by the girls in our class, an adulation that he received with equanimity. Looking back, I am, in a way, surprised that Mile and Toma took me into their confidence, considering my prevailing reputation as a bore who was not even a nerd. My friendship with them brought me into contact with the girls in the class, who had little regard for me. I was a consummate patsy in their eyes.

Most of our teachers were not Communist Party members. The high school curriculum included eight years of compulsory Russian language. No other foreign languages were taught. Our national history was distorted. Everything that occurred through the centuries pertaining to Serbian history was castigated as a sequence of evil and reckless wanton and thus relegated to footnotes at best. Instead, we were imbued with details of the Communist partisan struggle against the Nazis, a truly epic story but only a fraction of our nation's history. Other resistance groups that fought the Nazis during the war were either overlooked or branded as a bunch of traitors. This included the Serbian royalist guerillas who fought the Nazis valiantly while at the same time providing refuge in the mountains of western Serbia to downed American aviators.

It was during my high school years that my parents decided I should be introduced anew to the English language. There was an Englishman, Mr. Arthur Warren, in Novi Sad, the provincial capital, who gave English lessons. Mr. Warren was a tall and gaunt gentleman who always wore a gray suit, a vest, and a tie, even in the throes of summer. He had an aristocratic streak in him; why, he even inhaled when saying the word *yes*. He was always cordial yet reserved, his elongated face accentuated by a subtly quizzical and perhaps also mocking expression. He parted his silver hair neatly on the side à la Errol Flynn. I am mentioning this because his appearance and conduct were completely incongruous with his surroundings. He lodged in a small, dark, and damp courtyard apartment that always smelled of burned cooking fat. Mr. Warren's landlady was a Hungarian widow and former cook whose ubiquitous apron always sported the remnants of at least ten previous meals. In stark contrast to her tenant, she was short and plump and had cheeks that always appeared flushed. I still wonder what this oh-so-proper Brit was doing in such surroundings. For all I know, he could have been there in a clandestine capacity, or perhaps, considering the regime in Yugoslavia at the time, he might have been an exiled

British Communist. In any event, he labored diligently to make my efforts at learning English worthwhile, a difficult task since I skipped a number of lessons, preferring instead to surrender to my pervasive feeling of loneliness as I roamed aimlessly through the streets of Novi Sad. Later on, as a medical student, I continued to improve my command of English by attending evening classes at the British Cultural Council in Belgrade.

TRAGEDY STRIKES

My two older sisters were close. In contrast to her older sister, Evelyn, nicknamed Biba, who was a strong-willed, daring, and exuberant young lady, Isidora (my parents called her Pupa) was a quiet, mostly shy, and self-effacing girl of medium height with a shock of shoulder-length chestnut-color hair framing a broad, pale face, upon which perched a somewhat wider than aesthetically pleasing nose. Her large and deeply set eyes gave one the impression of melancholy and, at times, utter sadness. Upon finishing high school, Pupa enrolled in the School of Architecture in Belgrade, where she roomed with my mother's younger brother and his family. Since my parents were left destitute after the war, my maternal uncle Branko and aunt, both single and better off than my parents, supported Pupa, as they did me, by paying her tuition and providing her with pocket money. Pupa was not a stellar student and seemed to lack the drive to succeed. Her grades were accordingly less than satisfactory, and she failed a few courses, evoking displeasure in our parents and relatives.

There was a young man in town, also a university student, who had a dark, almost perennially suntanned complexion with a peculiar but appealing redness to his cheeks. He was of medium height, slender, and athletic. He was soft-spoken yet a persistent type of a fellow. His unnaturally pale green eyes were seemingly gently inviting at first glance but also devilish and condescending, giving him a Mephistophelian look. On the surface, he behaved gentlemanly yet somehow did not seem trustworthy. I am not sure how my sister got to know him. A relationship ensued; letters professing love were exchanged, and they frequently got together, all to the displeasure of our parents. We do not talk much about this in the Ciric family, as if silence would heal, when it only ignores the pain. It is true that depression can be genetically predisposed. It is also true, however, that the vicissitudes of life, so abundant after four years of a hideous war followed by the harshness of the Communist regime, with its seamy innuendos, false accusations, and sheer oppression, can adversely influence family relationships and thus bring terror and inconsolable grief to a fragile soul. So it was in February of 1955 that Pupa's melancholy became more apparent. On a cloudy and, for February, mild wintry day, I saw my sister walking up the gravel path toward the portal of the house, unusually lightly clad in a chiffon red-and-blue patterned dress, without a coat but with a shawl around her neck and with white knitted gloves on her hands. She seemed to look down as she walked, as if in deep thought. I called her from my bedroom window to ask if she should not put on her coat and to see where she was heading. The rattle of a passing train some four hundred yards away drowned my voice, and she did not respond. In a moment, she was in the portal and gone.

My parents were concerned when my sister did not come home that evening. Police were notified. Our good neighbors helped in the search. My sister was found next to the rail tracks just south of town. At the funeral, my father gave the eulogy at the cemetery. It was a moving speech; my father took the sole blame for the loss of his "dear angel," as he called her, absolving thereby any guilt that might have weighed heavily on the shoulders and in the hearts of others. He did so even though he was the only one who'd never reproached her and who'd loved her with all the tenderness of paternal love. Toma Rosandic, a famous Yugoslav sculptor and a friend of my father, created Pupa's gravestone, which bears her likeness holding a broken stem of a rose. I suspect my father made the sculptor aware of Pupa's last musings, when she left a written message quoting the seventeenth-century English Cavalier poet Robert Herrick:

Gather ye rosebuds while ye may
Old time is still a-flying;
And this same flower that smiles today
Tomorrow will be dying.

My father passed away a few short years later. Having lost her child, my mother opened the doors to our home to all who sought love, comfort, and solace, which they found in abundance on her shoulders. In time, she became the mother of the whole town. She invited writers and poets who frequented our town and enjoyed leaving the hustle and bustle of Belgrade to spend an evening in our home with a fine meal prepared by my mother, which included Riesling from my aunt's cellar, served in crystal decanters left over from the good times, to brighten the spirits and loosen the tongue. As for my siblings and me, our sister's abdication of life has left us with lingering questions in an unanswered search for closure.

HELLO, MEDICAL SCHOOL

Since the intermediate step of a liberal arts college is not a required path to enter a law or medical school in the continental European educational system, from high school, I was off to medical school. As I had no special proclivity toward biological sciences, the choice of a life in medicine was influenced largely by fond childhood memories of the town physician, Dr. Maksimovich. The good doctor was adored by the townsfolk not only as a healer, for he saved many a life, including my own when I came down with typhoid fever as a seven-year-old lad, but also as a man of infinite kindness and unbending honesty. A true Chekhovian character with rosy cheeks and pale blue eyes twinkling behind a pince-nez, he was always elegantly clad in a pin-striped gray suit in the winter, wearing the signature bow tie, and a white linen suit with a boater covering his baldness in the heat of summer. He was always welcome at the sick bed, for his bedside manner was impeccable as he dispensed care with a somewhat-raspy but reassuring voice. Dr. Maksimovich's fees were reasonable, or none if the patient was indigent. The poor man perished together with many other Serbs, Jews, and Romas in the Croatian Nazi concentration camp at Jasenovac.

In medical school, my high school nonchalance toward the matters of serious intellectual pursuits gradually gave way to a newfound interest in the wonders of—and also the many failings of—the medical arts and sciences. The first two years of medical school were devoted to basic sciences. I studied hard, as I felt a responsibility toward my parents, aunt, and uncle, for I was aware of their sacrifices in offering my sisters and me a higher education. They used all their resources to that end and never thought of spending their meager incomes on themselves for a vacation, clothes, or whatever. I passed exams from year to year, piling up highest marks, and this trend continued till my graduation as the valedictorian with the perfect average score of ten. I suppose taking exams is, to some degree, a matter of momentum. It is also possible that the professors who heard that there was a fellow trying to establish an unprecedented record without a blemish somehow rooted for me. I cherished then, and still do today, my professors. Professor Stefanovic was an imposing figure, tall and lanky, who kept his chin high without being haughty. His blue eyes were inquisitive, and he had a touch of almost boyish annoyance in his gaze. He was a highly regarded hematologist and educator. Professor Kosanovic, chief of general surgery, was a hulk of a man. He was uncompromising at first glance but was a gentle operator and a good steward of his department. He operated on me for a ruptured appendix when I was a freshman medical student. There were other distinguished professors who excelled as educators, including my professors of anatomy, Shljivic and Radojevic; Professor Todorovich, a world-renowned infectologist; Professor Ristic, chief of neurology; Professor Ilic, chief of dermatology; and many more. All were impressive educators who led by example.

Life as a medical student naturally revolved around going to classes, studying, and passing exams. I still remember the unpleasantness of being cold and having wet feet as I struggled to class, fighting the famous late-fall Belgrade *Koshava* wind and rain, and of studying in a cold room with my coat on in the dead of winter, when Belgrade becomes draped in white from the usual heavy snowfall. The Belgrade spring, with its warming sunshine and blue skies, would arrive in late April and be in full, rejuvenating force by May, when the palpable balminess persisted late into the night. The beauty of the lush greenery and the all-pervasive fragrance of the blooming linden trees lining the streets and squares in Belgrade in late May were always welcome, for they lifted students' spirits just in time for the final exams. I roomed with my older sister Biba in a quiet street lined with linden and chestnut trees, in a turn-of-the-century single-family home run down on the outside by the ravages of war but splendidly appointed with Victorian and other antique accoutrements on the inside. Biba, a resolute woman with presence, pursued a degree in English and other Germanic languages en route to a successful career as a translator. Self-assured of her good looks, she carries her slender and attractive frame with imperious abandon; Biba can be socially engaging but also intolerant of other people's viewpoints if they do not conform to her ideas and preferences.

It is a commonly accepted adage that university students tend to be liberal and have progressive views on social issues and public policy. This was not so in postwar Belgrade, where the student body was divided into two camps. The smaller one consisted of card-carrying members of the Communist party who proselytized their credo through haranguing platitudes at compulsory meetings for all students, and the much larger one, to which I belonged, consisted of anti-Communist and antisocialist believers in freedom and in self-reliance in bettering one's station in life without interference by the regime. We were also fun-loving students who yearned for all things Western and all that the American way of life had to offer. Of course, expressing these proclivities openly under the ever-watchful eyes of the Communist party on campus would have brought seriously unpleasant consequences. In a way, our anti-Communist gestalt was naive, as we hailed every setback of Communism and of dialectic materialism in the West. It is not surprising, therefore, that it took some time for those of us who grew to maturity under the Communist regime to intellectually recognize the true meaning of liberty and liberalism as we reached the free world, although the memory of the deceitful trickery of the Communist utopia remains imprinted on an emotional level.

My first encounter with the concrete (rather than imaginary) meaning of freedom and liberal thought was in 1956, when I spent six weeks as an exchange student in the small central Dutch city of Meppel. I was fortunate to be the houseguest of a well-respected local pediatrician, Guus Kleibeuker, and his wife, Bertha. Guus was a kind, mild-mannered, soft-spoken, analytical man who shone many a light on my incessant questions as to freedom, liberty, and the way of life under the capitalist system of governance. I shall always remember with great fondness this highly principled and frugal man who taught me not only the fundamentals of pediatric illnesses but also the appropriate bedside manner with his unhurried, gentle, compassionate, and always-uncompromising professionalism. More than forty years later, on the occasion of a neurosurgeons' conference in Amsterdam, I visited Guus, who, at ninety, remained elegantly erect, with his pale blue eyes still exuding an unspoken message of comfort and trust.

In medical school, I established lifelong friendships with a number of my colleagues. During parties staged in their homes, I got acquainted with young ladies, some of whom I dated. These were relatively innocent dates since overt promiscuity was not en vogue. An intimate relationship was a matter of courtship and trust, always with an eye on the consequences and the future. Maybe we were the last wave of the abstemious youth, although we tried to act like our heroes from the 1950s movies—Jimmy Stewart, Gregory Peck, Montgomery Clift, or, on a day when feeling especially macho, Marlon Brando, to mention but a few of my idols. One of my dates, whom I shall call M, was tall yet definitely not willowy. She was quiet and contemplative and had large, somewhat-sad hazel eyes set wide apart in a round face under a relatively low forehead. Her eyes gave the impression of being perpetually a touch surprised. She walked like a model on a dais, perhaps the result of an upbringing in a finishing school before the family fell on hard times. Some time into our relationship, I found the courage to take her to meet my mother at our home in Sremski Karlovci. My mother took an almost instant dislike to her, and the Sunday lunch turned into a strained scene, to say the least. We saw each other often, spending time mostly walking around Belgrade; I occasionally took her out for dinner, mostly where they served grilled cheese sandwiches. I pretended that grilled cheese was my favorite food, though in fact, it was all I could afford on my meager student allowance. I presume M was aware of my pecuniary want, although she never let me know, and she acted as if I were the most generous companion. We parted when she received a scholarship for a year in England, and we never saw each other again.

Shortly thereafter, I met B, a tall and slender beauty with raven hair, a domineering attitude, and a bearing typical of women who are aware of their remarkable appearance. I was quite smitten by her and proud when she would allow me to parade her at parties, all dressed up, usually in sophisticated black dresses. She was also quite secretive. I never got to know her well; in fact, she never told me her surname. She refused to let me take her home, lest I find out where she lived. I never found out anything about her background, where she hailed from, her family, or what she did for living, yet we managed to see each other for almost a year before she vanished as suddenly as she had appeared in my life. Looking back, I wonder if she was in the service of the government, seeking out and reporting on potentially anti-Communist students.

There were a few others with whom I went out, to use the Belgrade jargon for dating at that time, including the daughter (a few years my senior) of an impoverished Belgrade industrialist with a grand apartment in central Belgrade. She was mostly my opera date. Another date was a well-connected young lady whose father was a general in the army and who lived half a block away from my lodgings, an important dating detail in those times of precarious transportation by tram or—preferably, for pecuniary reasons—by foot.

I decided on neurosurgery as my life's work late in my senior year. During my clinical rotation in neurosurgery, I became intrigued by the many secrets locked in our central nervous system and by the imponderables of healing brain diseases with surgery. The eloquent and enticing lectures by the chairman of the department of neurosurgery, Dr. Slobodan Kostic, a gentleman and a consummate connoisseur of life, also contributed to my decision. Looking back, there might have been another, though less transparent, reason. In order to overcome their inherent insecurities, many neurosurgeons (including myself) might have chosen this difficult surgical specialty knowing that they would be challenged every step of the way and that the field requires an undivided commitment and lifelong consecrated effort if they are to succeed and advance the field. However, it was not to be. In spite of being the valedictorian, I was denied specialization by the Communist Party–dominated university administration. I received my diploma in March 1958; since the compulsory conscription into the military service was not due until October, I decided to give it a try abroad in the interim without any preconceived ideas as to my long-term future. It was through sheer serendipity that I landed as an intern in the department of general surgery in Mannheim, Germany, under Dr. Wilhelm Gokel, a surgical genius and an exacting man.

In October of 1958, I returned to Belgrade and entered the Medical Officers Military School, where I received compulsory basic military training before being promoted to lieutenant. My initial assignment was to serve as a military physician in southern Serbia, attached to a cavalry unit. The barracks I shared with the noncommissioned officers were infested with rats. To be safe at night, the legs of our beds were set within containers filled with water. Most of the remaining months of my service were spent in an outpatient military clinic in Belgrade. This was a cushy assignment, as I was able to stay overnight at the apartment I shared with my sister. I also took pleasure in cavorting after work at the beach on the Sava River. The carefree life of a beach bum ended when, at the end of the summer, I received the invitation to return to my general surgery mentor in Germany, albeit this time as a resident.

THE JOURNEY BEGINS

My mother had a longing look in her eyes, pleading that I might change my decision to leave and seek my future abroad—an uncertain future beyond the immediate appointment as a resident in general surgery at a Catholic hospital in Mannheim, Germany. I suppose her motherly instincts told her I was leaving for good. The look in her eyes on that drizzly and unusually warm late-December evening in 1959, as the train was about to leave the Belgrade station and take me on the journey of my life, would remain indelibly imprinted in my soul. The poignancy of the scene grew more vivid in time, as I gradually realized how heartbroken my mother must have been not only because she was losing her son but also because she knew that the family traditions carried over from generation to generation, so important to a Serbian family, were about to be extinguished for good. Thus, at the very beginning of the new life I was seeking, I felt the first pang of guilt and sadness, for I was perhaps selfishly abandoning my mother, my family, and my ancestral home.

The overnight trip to Mannheim was spent in listless thoughts and soul-searching doubts. *Oh well*, I thought, *if I do not like it abroad, I'll find my way back; hopefully, I will be able to save enough for that contingency.* My stipulated stipend as resident was a measly 100 DM a month. "Well," the mother superior of the St. Hedwig Clinic told me when I broached the subject of compensation, "you are getting free room and board; that is worth something, isn't it?" The experience in Mannheim, though, was invaluable not only for setting the foundation for a crisp, precise, and bloodless German-style surgical technique reminiscent of anatomic dissections but also as a superb way to learn how to take it on the chin. After the miniglory of being the valedictorian at the Belgrade Medical School, I found myself back in the lion's den of *Chefarzt* Wilhelm Gokel. At operations, he used to assail his residents with all kinds of colorful and egregiously offending epithets, especially when they were foreigners. "Your clumsiness is killing my patient!" he would scream with relish. Yet I had the feeling he made his pronouncements not to offend but in jest, for he delighted in being politically incorrect. He also had mellower moments, when he would say, "Ciric, I can buy you a Steinway piano, but you will never be Arthur Rubinstein." Today, decades after the barrage of harangues by Dr. Gokel, I feel that in some ways, the harshness of the ambiance surrounding the otherwise-superb training in general surgery I received from this brusque but good-hearted man was another positive experience that helped strengthen my tolerance to such less-than-hospitable future circumstances. After two years of accelerated surgical education, I earned my stripes when the chief left me in charge of his practice as he embarked on an extended vacation. Professionally and personally, I felt vindicated running a busy department and being in charge of a formidable surgical schedule that included appendectomies, hernia repairs, and a smattering of gall bladder removals. Just as was the custom with the chief, in between cases, the nuns served me and my assistant tea and sandwiches. In the afternoons, I would cycle to my chief's office to see new patients. Looking back, I am still amazed that the chief had so much trust in me that he turned over his practice to a novice surgeon who as yet had not passed the necessary exams for accreditation as a general surgeon. I also remember this period in my professional life with fondness, for it was then that I fell passionately in love with my future bride, Anne, who has been at my side for more than fifty years.

ANNE

Meeting Anne was truly a chance encounter. It would have never happened but for a spur-of-the-moment suggestion by my intern at the St. Hedwig's Clinic in Mannheim, Franz Biedermann, to join him for a Saturday day trip to Baden-Baden. Franz was engaged to Anne's sister Edith and probably wanted to show off his fiancée. As the chief resident in general surgery, I had to make myself available at the St. Hedwig Clinic around the clock, literally living in the hospital, so I had nearly no free time, for in those days, the current concept of resident hour restrictions was not known. I accepted the invitation after arranging for coverage with a colleague from the department of gynecology and obstetrics.

I looked forward to the opportunity to spend an afternoon in what I knew from hearsay to be a lovely city in the foothills of the Black Forest and a historical playground of European royalty, aristocracy, and an assortment of intellectual celebrities, including Turgenev and Dostoyevsky. According to the Baden-Baden gossip, Dostoyevsky lost his last ruble in the city's gilded casino and, in order to pay his rent, reportedly had to pawn his wife's wedding dress. During the short train ride from Mannheim to Baden-Baden, I was entertained by Franz's antics and jokes, told in the nearly impossible-to-understand local Baden accent.

It was a sunny early fall day in Baden-Baden, when the oak trees along the promenades began to shed their leaves, covering the grassy embankments and promenades along the Oos River with myriad shades of red and gold. The city was bustling with human activities; some were simply walking and window-shopping, and others were enjoying coffee and delicious pastries. Relaxed by the pleasing scene surrounding me, I followed Franz into the Schneyer family's upscale clothing store in the center of the city. Anne was right there to greet us. As my gaze met hers, I felt a peculiar sensation, a mixture of admiration for the beauty of this statuesque brunette and a contagious calmness emanating from Anne's serene demeanor. I was also enthralled by the warmth of her hazel eyes, which were set in a perfectly oval face, separated by a nose more Greek than Germanic, and framed by a shock of naturally wavy shoulder-length hair. The spectacles she sported and the trim, simply cut gray dress she wore, accentuating her bust over a slender waist, added to the aura of a spirited vibrancy and feminine invincibility. As we were introduced to each other, I also noticed a hint of naughty devilishness as Anne rendered a half smile revealing symmetrically placed, cute dimples on either side of her not-too-prominent lips, conveying not only love of life but also determination and self-restraint. I could not take my gaze off the face of this remarkable woman. I suppose I stuttered and blushed when she addressed me with the usual German "Herr Doctor" and engaged me in a conversation that I suspect was designed to test my intellectual sagacity, cultural acumen, and societal civility. I probably failed on all three scores, for all I could muster was an argumentative, contentious demeanor in an attempt to hide my skin-deep grasp of a whole array of humanities' intellectual and artistic accomplishments that I somehow clumsily managed to stumble into during our conversation. Nevertheless, I evidently sparked at least a trifle of interest in Anne, as later that evening, during a dinner in a rustic restaurant surrounded by vineyards, she agreed to my invitation to meet again. So began the romance that was to endure for the rest of our lives.

NEUROSURGERY RESIDENCY IN GERMANY

In pursuit of my professional goal, I subsequently applied to the Max Planck Brain Research Institute and was accepted as a fellow to the neurosurgical department of the University of Cologne, under the leadership Wilhelm Toennis, who was one of the leading neurosurgeons in Europe at the time. The change from Mannheim, where I'd advanced relatively rapidly to being the number-two man in the department of general surgery, to being "And who are you?" in the department of neurosurgery in Cologne was like a fall down Niagara Falls—I went from something to nothing. Professor Toennis was larger than life, a king in his domain. The neurosurgery department was housed in a self-standing building with its own ancillary divisions, such as pathology, radiology, and research facilities of the Max Planck Institute.

The government-financed health care in Germany at the time favored a two-tiered medicine. For those insured through general insurance, there were wards with six to eight beds. The informed consent for a brain operation on such a ward was rather laconic. It consisted of the professor acknowledging the patient and family with a curt nod, followed by making remarks addressed chiefly to the assembled retinue of assistant residents while pointing with his index finger to where they should make the incision. He would tell them how to proceed with the craniotomy, what to watch for, and similar technical details. Meanwhile, the patient would squirm, and his or her eyes would start rolling, half out of fear and uncertainty as to what all this gibberish by the professor meant and half out of awe at having been touched personally by the great man.

In contrast, patients with private insurance were housed on a separate ward, in private rooms with all sorts of amenities, including daily fresh flowers. Only one resident assistant, usually chosen by the professor's wife, had the privilege of helping the professor on the private ward, where patients were addressed with "my lady" and "sir." It is also remarkable that only the professor had the government-sanctioned privilege of billing patients with private insurance, while his residents, some of whom were in the department for as long as twenty years, were full-time salaried physicians. The assistant residents did not have the opportunity to branch off on their own until released by the professor and until a university chair opened in one of the neurosurgery centers in Germany. In the operating room, the second assistant was not allowed to talk directly to the professor, lest he be reprimanded. Rather, he had to address his remarks and questions to the first assistant, who would then convey them to the professor. All publications had to include the professor's name as one of the leading authors. I should also mention that the professor took a nap in his sanctuary every afternoon, guarded by an impenetrable blonde Westphalia-born *Walkure* handmaiden.

As for my colleagues in the department, most of them were

supportive enough to ease the heavy burden of being on the lowest level of the hierarchical totem pole in the department of neurosurgery. There were also a few obsequious acolytes. They ingratiated themselves by helping the professor into his lab coat; carrying his briefcase; and, as the ultimate in servility, hiding from the professor the bad news concerning his patients' progress on the morning rounds. Yet Professor Toennis was a fine academic mentor, as every resident had to write a doctoral thesis. The dual appointment as a junior resident and a fellow at the Brain Research Institute enabled me to complete and, subsequently, successfully defend my thesis on identifying reasons for failure to diagnose brain tumors early enough, when they are still treatable. This thesis would be obsolete by today's imaging standards, when patients with early symptoms of a brain tumor are screened with either computed tomography (CT) or magnetic resonance imaging (MRI).

Overall, my neurosurgical training in Cologne was a positive experience that culminated in an invitation from the second-ranking member in the department, Professor Marguth, to join his team upon Dr. Marguth's appointment as the professor and chair of neurosurgery at the University of Munich. As it turned out, I decided against staying in Germany.

ROMANCE AND WEDDING

For about two years, Anne and I met nearly every weekend. Occasionally, I would find a free day and take the train to Baden-Baden, but mostly, Anne came to Mannheim and later, as I began my neurosurgery residency, to Cologne. I remember pacing the platform of the train station, waiting for Anne to arrive, feverish with anticipation, only to experience a feeling of relief when I saw Anne alight from the train—always in a great mood, upbeat, and sophisticated in appearance and demeanor. During those blissful weekends, we would take long drives in my VW Bug along the west bank of the Rhine Valley and sample local food in quaint inns before heading back to Cologne by country roads east of the Rhine. The inns we frequented, overlooking the river or at some distance from the river, surrounded by the dense and foreboding forests of the relatively sparsely populated Eifel region, offered an enchanting setting for a romance and for a quiet respite away from the usual boisterousness of the urban living in Cologne. The Rhine, though not as stately as the Danube, appears to languish in some parts, tame and tired, with a calm pewter-tinted surface, while in other places, especially around Koblenz, it churns, beating the rocky shores with powerful white waves. The Rhine Valley winds tortuously through a hilly countryside studded with vineyards that slope steeply down to the river, guarded by medieval castles perched on top of the hill. Legend says that the bellicose masters of the castles would swoop down on their stallions from their lofts in the sky and pounce on the weary travelers trekking up and down the river in the valley. According to ancient Germanic lore, on the crest of one of the steepest and craggiest rocks on the eastern bank of the river sat an alluring siren, Lorelei, who caused shipwrecks by distracting the voyaging river captains with her mellifluous songs while combing her golden hair.

After a carefree, halcyon romance, the time came for life-determining decisions, both in our relationship and in regard to our future. The former was reached without much being spoken, as we gradually slid into the realization that our lives were destined to be shared.

The wedding took place in the Russian church in Wiesbaden with all the accoutrements of the Christian Orthodox tradition, including crowns for the bridal pair, walking three times around the front of the altar, incense, and pious chanting by the priests. There was no pomp or white bridal dress, let alone a bridal train, and not even an officially designated professional photographer—all because of my insecure trepidations. Still, my dear Anne was the most beautiful, elegant, and graceful bride in her body-conscious creamy white attire adorned with an understated fur collar. The reception was in the Hotel Rose in Wiesbaden, an elegant establishment, albeit from a somewhat-bygone era. In all, there were only seventeen persons present, indeed a small wedding. Our honeymoon trip took us first to Fuessen, a sleepy Bavarian alpine village, where we hiked, enjoyed hearty Bavarian food, and retired early in suspense of a blissful night as a gurgling and rippling stream, glittering under the full moon, cascaded out of a dense forest of birch, oak, and fir trees a stone's throw from our window. From there, it was off to the country of song and love. After a night in Rome, where we enjoyed the proximity of our hotel to the Piazza del Popolo, we headed south to Gaeta and Terracina, two sleepy fishing villages where the glittering horizon of the Mediterranean blends imperceptibly with the distant azure sky. We enjoyed watching the fiery magnificence of the setting sun as it straddled the horizon before surrendering to the splendor of the star-studded night. A dinner in the local trattoria under a canopy of vines will also always be remembered with fondness. With the honeymoon over, we went back to the harsh reality of facing our future.

LEAVING FOR THE PROMISED LAND

Most Americans, save for those who call this continent their ancestral land, have a unique story to tell of their ancestors coming to these shores. These might be stories of religious persecution and pious pilgrimage, as set forth in William Bradford's account *Of Plymouth Plantation*, or stories of ethnic torment, as rendered in Mary Antin's masterpiece *The Promised Land*. These could also be chronicles of poverty and hunger that drove untold thousands to seek a new life in this country, or they might be narratives of pioneering spirits and even of restless adventurism. Let us also never forget those who were forcefully brought to the Americas against their will, for we owe them not only our deepest respect but also a place in our hearts forever and always. Then there are more nuanced stories with no single calamitous circumstance but, rather, a sequence of propitious or inimical events that incrementally led to the decision to turn off the ancient light and leave the nest where our characters and values were sculpted to head for an uncertain future.

After two years of residency under Professor Toennis, I had to decide whether I would want to spend the rest of my life in Germany. Dr. Marguth's invitation to join him in Munich was appealing for a number of reasons, not the least of which was that I held Professor Marguth in highest esteem and that joining him at the prestigious University of Munich would open the doors to a potentially successful career in Germany. However, after some deliberation, I concluded that staying in Germany was not something I would be comfortable with. I suppose the memories of the horrid experiences that befell my family and my nation during the Second World War influenced my decision. At the same time, for a number of reasons, I also eschewed going back to Communist Yugoslavia. After some soul searching, Anne and I decided to leave Europe for the United States.

I applied to several neurosurgery residency programs in the United States. It took some courage to ask for a meeting with Professor Toennis and to tell him of my decision. He graciously took the news; remarked that he was on familiar terms with legendary Chicago neurosurgeon Dr. Paul Bucy at Chicago Wesley Memorial Hospital, a Northwestern University–affiliated institution; and offered to write me a letter of recommendation. Propitiously, Dr. Bucy had an open resident position, and I was accepted. I am confident, though, that the letter of recommendation from the leading European neurosurgeon was instrumental in advancing my cause.

The immigration laws at the time favored immigrants from Western Europe. Immigration applicants from Eastern Europe, including those from Communist Yugoslavia, had to wait a long time to receive their immigration papers. Since I was born in Vienna (another of my mother's idiosyncrasies, as she did not trust Serbian obstetricians), in accordance with the US laws, I was classified as hailing from Austria. Being married to a German citizen was also helpful to that end. The US consul in

Frankfurt who signed my immigration papers, a Harvard type wearing a tweed jacket with leather elbow patches and preppy crimson socks showing below his too-short khaki pants, surprised me with his detailed knowledge of my past. I was amazed and duly impressed. In retrospect, such masterful Cold War vigilance, unfortunately, must have deteriorated leading up to 9/11.

I was apprehensive as we flew on Pan Am to New York, for I was trading a potentially promising future in the Old World for an uncertainty awaiting me in the United States. As we arrived, the welcome mat was spread by a friend of Anne's mother, a wealthy widow of the songwriter Pat Ballard, who arranged for us to stay at the fabled St. Regis Hotel. As we arrived at the hotel, the doorman inquired about our luggage. It was only then that I realized I had left our luggage unclaimed at the airport. Ouch! I had to take one of the longest bus rides of my life back to the airport, where I was reminded mockingly and with a wagging forefinger by the officer on duty, "This is not really the best way to start life in this country." Be that as it may, looking back, I was a privileged immigrant in this magical promised land, for I had an education and a job lined up. I was ready to start from scratch and eager to prove myself.

After a couple of days of sightseeing in Manhattan and getting adjusted to the cultural shock imparted by this perpetually awake and agog metropolis, we were off to Chicago, where friends of Anne arranged for us to rent a room at 14 East Elm, a day hotel less than a stone's throw from Rush Street. On a crisp morning in May 1963, as the vastness of the heavens over Chicago began to pale with the sun rising over the glittering lake, I stepped out of the hotel on my way to the Chicago Wesley Memorial Hospital. Upon entering the cavernous portal of that iconic institution, I was greeted with chimes coming from high up in the vaulted ceiling. As I looked up in search of the origin of this solemn sound, my eyes came to rest on the inscription "Wesley Memorial Hospital, the Cathedral of Healing." For a moment, I hesitated in reverent obeisance before ascending to Dr. Bucy's twelfth-floor office, where I was met by his assistant, Rose Lotz, a kind and unpretentious person severely handicapped by the consequences of polio. She remained a true friend and confidante throughout my residency.

Soon Dr. Bucy came in as if flying, with his lab coat unfurled behind him and with his residents and students following in his wake. Dr. Bucy was a man of presence, albeit short in stature, for which he compensated with an erect and self-assured yet dignified posture. His exquisite diction, graceful fluency of speech delivered in a sonorous voice, and steely blue-gray eyes gazing straight at whomever he was addressing immediately commanded attention and respect without demanding it—a trait unique to individuals with leadership qualities. I was in awe of this man, for I knew he had received every honor neurosurgery can bestow on one of its own. As we exchanged greetings, I felt I should express my respect, as I would under similar circumstances in Europe, by offering to help Dr. Bucy out of his lab coat, only to be reproached that this was not necessary. I also presented him with my doctoral thesis from the University of Cologne, which he unceremoniously placed on the windowsill next to his desk, where it remained unopened until the completion of my residency four years later, when I quietly retrieved it. I realized later that Dr. Bucy was not disrespectful of my academic accomplishments. Instead, he wanted to judge me based on my performance as a resident rather than by my written thesis.

NEUROSURGERY RESIDENCY IN CHICAGO

The acquisition of knowledge and the accrual of surgical experience during a residency involve a gradual process, similar to putting a puzzle together until it is complete. As residents, we were asked to be present in Dr. Bucy's office when he took history and examined his patients, an invaluable experience in acquiring the necessary acumen of neurological and neurosurgical knowledge and in exercising proper judgment when placing surgical indications. Contrary to some other neurosurgery training programs, in which the residents are placed in the surgical arena early on in their training, Dr. Bucy believed in incremental assumption of independent surgical responsibility. This usually began with assisting the attending neurosurgeon, followed by performing parts of the operative procedure, such as the opening and closing of the operative field, and then performing the operation from beginning to end under Dr. Bucy's watchful supervision. In the senior year, the residents performed the operations independently, always with the understanding that Dr. Bucy, or whoever was the attending neurosurgeon, would be available at a moment's notice should the intraoperative situation demand his presence. Needless to say, the learning process is a lifelong endeavor that does not stop with the end of residency.

Neurosurgery residency is also a challenging physical effort. This was true more so in 1963 than now, considering the recently mandated restriction on the hours a resident can spend at work in the hospital. Since Dr. Bucy had only three residents and the senior resident did not take calls, the junior residents had to be on call every other night, during which there was always enough urgent work to complete so that sleep was in short supply. Oftentimes the night shift blended imperceptibly into the following day's routine duties, including assisting the attending neurosurgeons in the operating room during notoriously lengthy neurosurgical procedures. The patients scheduled for surgery were admitted late in the afternoon the day prior and sometimes several days ahead of surgery. This meant that the resident on call had to prepare for surgery—work up, in resident parlance—as many as seven to ten patients on any given evening. This involved writing in longhand a detailed history and recording a thorough neurologic examination. After completing the rounds and recording the salient facts from the newly admitted patients' histories and neurological findings, I would retire to the departmental offices on the twelfth floor of the old Wesley building late into the night to write my patients' stories, hoping not to be disturbed by a dreaded call from the emergency department. The spectacular nocturnal view of Chicago I enjoyed from my perch in Dr. Bucy's office, resplendent in scintillating lights yet seemingly gloriously at peace, was an inspiring backdrop that enhanced my desire to excel as a chronicler of my patients' woes and handicaps. This was a daunting task for a foreign-born resident whose command of

English might have been deficient when it came to writing cogently meaningful health records that were critical to the tasks at hand. To that end, I took cues from Dr. Bucy's papers and essays, recognized in the neurosurgical community for their graceful literary elegance and power of words.

My chief resident was a square-shouldered, self-confident Chicago native with a touch of stolid attitude whose upright bearing, crew cut, precise diction, and penchant for order and cleanliness were reminiscent of an officer in the marines, which, as I recall, he was not—although he ran the department and reigned over his residents as if he were one. I learned much from him, not only relative to neurosurgical techniques, but also in attitudes and relationships with the attending neurosurgeons and other healthcare providers. Over the years, we forged a close friendship, especially after he sought me out some thirty years later when he was in need of neurosurgical care himself. Fortunately, the surgical procedure succeeded in cementing our friendship. Being of service to a colleague neurosurgeon, as well as other colleagues and their families, has been one of the most distinct privileges of my professional career and one I have always cherished with humility.

The year I began my training at Northwestern, the second-year resident was a kind fellow who was at odds with the chief resident and eventually transferred to another training program somewhere in the east. This opened the door for me to advance the following year to the position of chief resident after only a year on the service. During the ensuing two years, the three recruited junior residents were a strapping, clear-thinking, dependable young midwesterner with blond hair; a somewhat-gangly but agreeable and witty easterner of

Welsh extraction with longish hair and an undulating gait; and a tall, slim, handsome, and somewhat-reticent southerner. All of them were highly intelligent, talented, eager to learn, and loyal to the core. I submit that keeping this interesting albeit diverse group of personalities focused over two years was a challenge.

We were housed along with other Wesley residents in a stately neoclassical building on Delaware Street, half a block east of Chicago's Magnificent Mile. The entrance hall featured all the usual trappings of a seriously upscale multistoried residence on or close to Michigan Avenue. The elegant green-and-brown fake Persian carpet matched in tone the dark wood-paneled walls, which were adorned with tapestries, and the carved wood-decorated ceiling. A massive oak table occupied the center of the hall, with chairs fit for King Arthur and his knights arranged tastefully along the walls. Off to the right of the entrance was Chez Paul, one of Chicago's iconic French restaurants, which catered to the city's *haute vole* and was out of reach for the meagerly compensated Wesley residents. Our apartment was large by the usual standards for resident quarters and strikingly bright thanks to large French windows facing East Delaware Street. The ten-foot-high ceilings added further to the feeling of bygone elegant spaciousness. At the end of a working day, sometimes close to midnight, I used to invite the intern or one of my junior residents to join Anne and me for a late supper prepared by Anne, who always waited for me with a silent understanding of my travails as a neurosurgery resident.

On rare days when I was off call and before our daughters were born, Anne and I would rent a car and explore Chicago's surroundings, admiring the lush greenery of the north suburbs, with their grand mansions, and the peaceful atmosphere of the magnificent Michigan sand dunes to the south. During my residency years in Chicago, Anne and I were blessed with the birth of our two daughters. Our eldest daughter was the cutest pumpkin of a baby. She was always in a good mood; rarely cried at night, as if she knew not to disturb her weary father, and she grew into a just-as-sweet toddler. She was excited with joy when her baby sister came into the world a mere thirteen months later.

Our second daughter showed from day one her proclivity toward a rapscallion agenda, not necessarily by crying at night, as infants tend to do, but, I am convinced, by crying when she absolutely wanted this or that. These strong-willed manifestations continued as she grew into a toddler and a preschooler, with outbursts such as prostrating herself on the floor in a fit of anger. The early childhood manifestations of a strong will gradually evolved into resolute, but also thoughtful leadership qualities. As they grew side by side, not only did the girls bond reminiscent of twins, but also, their natures and views blended. They excelled at school, became defenders of social justice, and became courageously albeit courteously assertive.

Upon arriving in the United States, Anne and I were greeted by Anne's childhood friend Alice and Alice's husband, Robert Marcy, an exiled Hungarian army officer and engineer. They were a childless couple who immigrated to the United States before us. Alice, who was our child's godmother, and Robert remained close and true friends for many years. The magical days, especially for our children, when Aunt Alice and Uncle Robert would join us for Thanksgiving and Christmas dinners will forever remain as some of the most joyous memories of our family life.

Considering that neurosurgery is as much an art as it is science and that it also requires critical wisdom and an abiding moral compass when passing judgment that can reflect irretrievably on an individual's destiny, it is clear that mentorship plays the pivotal role in the professional development of a neurosurgeon. Therefore, it might be appropriate to describe briefly my mentor's clinical and scientific interests, all of which he passed on to his disciples. Dr. Bucy had a special interest in the surgical treatment of brain tumors, both malignant and benign. In 1967, Dr. Bucy published in the *Journal of Neurosurgery* a seminal paper on the surgical removal of malignant brain tumors, in which he equated improved short- and long-term prognoses with the extent of tumor removal. A number of investigators, including the author of these memoirs, have since published similar results confirming Dr. Bucy's thesis in this regard. Dr. Bucy also relished operating on such benign tumors as meningiomas, pituitary gland tumors, and vestibular schwannomas.

In the science arena, Dr. Bucy's interest was in the field of motor functions. His research was based on the hypothesis that besides the main bundle of motor nerves in the brain and spinal cord, known as the pyramidal tract, there are also secondary extrapyramidal motor pathways. The research required surgical division of the pyramidal tract in primates, operations performed by the resident staff in Dr. Bucy's laboratory under the same stringent circumstances relative to anesthesia and sterility as in human brain surgery. The procedure required using a skull trephination the size of a quarter immediately above the animal's ear and sneaking under the temporal lobe until the upper brain stem, known as the midbrain, came into view. The next step was to identify two specific arteries, known by their anatomic acronyms as PCA and SCA, coursing parallel to each other across the bottom of the midbrain and then divide the pyramidal tract between them. These structures could be seen with one eye only, as they are at the end of a deep and dark surgical corridor.

One day it happened that the ear, nose, and throat residents were being instructed in the enjoining laboratory room on how to perform a middle-ear procedure on a cadaver head under the operating microscope. When I asked the chief resident why they needed a microscope, he replied, "Because, my friend, there is no living human being who has seen an eardrum with two eyes without the microscope. We prefer the clarity and safety of binocular vision during our operations."

I had the opportunity to peek through the optics of the microscope, only to be amazed by the details of the anatomy revealed—brilliantly illuminated, magnified, and seen with both eyes. *Hmm*, I thought. *Why don't I try to use the operating microscope during our laboratory procedures on the primates' brain stems?* So we did, and the microscope made the procedures much easier, for we could now execute our maneuvers in a brightly lit and magnified field under the comfort of binocular vision. It was only later that I found out why the operating microscope affords binocular vision: the objective lens splits the image into both oculars, no matter how tiny or deep the object is. How little did I anticipate at that moment the significant role the operating microscope and microsurgery would have in the future development of neurosurgery.

Dr. Bucy's study revealed that after the initial paralysis on the side opposite of the divided pyramidal tract, the animals would show a nice recovery of strength within a few weeks. This salutary course was attributed to the presence of extrapyramidal motor neuronal pathways. These experiments also explain the clinical observation of recovery of movements in the wake of an injury to the pyramidal tract, such as following a stroke. The recovered motor functions, though, are usually less coordinated and thus functionally less satisfactory, especially in older individuals, compared to the natural movements initiated by the pyramidal tract.

It is clear from these reminiscences that my neurosurgical education was at the hands of a mentor who had many roles. As a clinical mentor, Dr. Bucy taught his residents the importance of listening to the patient and performing a thorough neurologic examination, which are essential for securing a correct diagnosis. He was also the surgical preceptor, the scientific adviser, and, most importantly, the man who guided his residents on the new and unchartered path of neurosurgical ethics and its varied aspects, especially the respect for a life with dignity. Looking back, I am inclined to think that Dr. Bucy endowed his residents with solid academic and surgical foundations so that they were capable, long after his passing, of excelling in the subspecialty areas he did not teach them.

Other attending neurosurgeons on the Wesley staff also participated in resident education. Dr. Bucy's associate, Dr. Robert Oberhill, was a bear of a man who was a gifted though disillusioned neurosurgeon. He made early rounds, around five in the morning, and preferred to leave the hospital after scheduled surgery, which was usually before lunch. The resident staff attributed Dr. Oberhill's lack of enthusiasm to his being consigned to Dr. Bucy's shadow, if not completely sidelined by the boss. Yet the residents learned a lot from this gruff-appearing but fair and true-to-his-word man.

Dr. Dan Ruge, on the other hand, was a tall, silver-haired, and somewhat-taciturn gentleman who was always elegantly clad and was also one of the ushers at the iconic Fourth Presbyterian Church on the Magnificent Mile in Chicago. He was socially well connected through his mentor, Dr. Loyal Davis, who was the chair of the department of surgery at Northwestern and the division of neurosurgery at Passavant Memorial Hospital, across the street from Wesley. Dr. Ruge, a skilled and compellingly neat spine surgeon, commanded a high-end practice with captains of industry and an assortment of Chicago's *haute vole* as his patients. He used to round daily on the sixteenth floor of the Wesley Memorial Hospital, where VIP patients were housed, even on days when he had no patients of his own on that floor. When, after several weeks of tagging along, I gathered the courage to inquire why we were making rounds on this floor on days when we had no patients there, Dr. Ruge retorted, "Well, son, this is just why." Dr. Loyal Davis, President Reagan's father-in-law, was instrumental in Dr. Ruge's future appointment as President Reagan's personal physician. This proved to be a providential choice, as Dr. Ruge (along with the Secret Service detail) assisted in saving President Reagan's life after the assassination attempt by agreeing that the motorcade be diverted to the nearby George Washington Medical Center instead of having it proceed to the Georgetown University Hospital, as designated by protocol.

The last six months of my residency were spent at the Veterans Administration Hospital, kitty-corner from Wesley. As the chief resident, I was in charge of the neurosurgical service. My nominal preceptors during that period were Dr. Ruge and Dr. Nicholas Wetzel. Dr. Wetzel was a quiet man of few words but also was studious and a talented and fearless operator who relished tackling difficult cases. Dr. Wetzel, also a Loyal Davis disciple, was disinclined toward Dr. Bucy, whom he considered an intruder on the Northwestern neurosurgical turf. The professional rivalry between Dr. Loyal Davis and Dr. Bucy blossomed when Dr. Bucy was appointed chief of neurosurgery at the Wesley Memorial Hospital, which, up until that time, was the exclusive domain of Dr. Davis and his staff. This rivalry had national repercussions in that both Dr. Davis and Dr. Bucy were granted neurosurgery residency programs by the neurosurgery governing board, even though the two institutions were across the street from each other on the Northwestern Medical School campus. As the chief resident at the VA hospital, I bridged the divide between the two neurosurgery powerhouses. I was respectful to both, but my primary allegiance was to Dr. Bucy. During my tenure at the VA hospital, Dr. Davis retired, and Dr. Bucy took over the leadership of the combined services and residency programs.

LISTEN TO THE PATIENT

At the time of my residency, neurosurgery was an evolving specialty lacking the current sophistication in diagnostic tools and neurosurgical technology. Hence, the diagnosis of brain tumors and other intracranial lesions was hampered by the absence of reliable noninvasive imaging studies. Skull radiographs, of course, were available, but they showed only skull-related pathologies (for example, a skull fracture), evidence of a skull lesion (such as an erosion due to an underlying expansive but otherwise-invisible process), or signs of an infection or skull tumor. Cerebral angiography was also available, during which an iodinated contrast material was injected directly into the carotid or vertebral arteries in the neck so as to visualize the intracranial arteries and veins. In some patients, a malignant or benign tumor would become visible on the angiogram, while in others, tumor location could be deduced indirectly based on the distortion of the normal arterial or venous vessel anatomy. As this is an invasive study, it is not without risk, especially of causing a stroke. The same can be said for the pneumoencephalogram—by today's imaging standards, an obsolete, invasive, and painful study during which air was injected into the spinal column in an awake and usually sitting patient. The injected air would ascend through the spinal column into the head, where it would outline the structure of the brain, both outside as it approximated the skull as well as inside the brain by entering into the natural brain cavities (cerebral ventricles). Again, based on the distortion of the normal anatomy, the neurosurgeon was able to surmise the location of a brain lesion, such as a tumor or other space-occupying lesions. Alternately, the air could also be introduced directly into the cerebral ventricles via a bur hole in the skull, which required a surgical procedure. Clearly, neither study was resorted to lightly.

Midway in my residency, a new imaging study became available. This was the radionuclide brain scan, during which a radioactive compound, technetium-99, was injected intravenously. Due to the physiologic impenetrability of the blood-brain barrier, the radioactive material does not penetrate into the brain parenchyma. Conversely, when the blood-brain barrier is broken down, as, for example, by an intracranial tumor, be it benign or malignant, the radioactive material penetrates into the tumor, outlining its position in the brain. This was the first significant noninvasive imaging advancement.

It is not surprising, therefore, that in the early 1960s, the diagnosis of an intracranial tumor and of a whole array of neurologic illnesses was still dependent on a detailed history and thorough neurologic examination. It has been known since time immemorial that listening to the patient's history reveals the nature of an illness, for each illness leaves a specific footprint—that is, a specific set of symptoms—and that the bedside examination localizes the site of the pathology. Of course, it stands to reason that in order to make sense out of the patient's history, a thorough familiarity with a wide spectrum of neurologic illnesses is an essential prerequisite. For example, strokes tend to occur precipitously, while brain tumors evolve gradually and tend to progress more insidiously unless the presenting symptom is an epileptic seizure or the tumor is a highly malignant brain cancer, but even then, the symptoms usually evolve within a matter of days or weeks rather than acutely over a period of seconds or minutes. In fact, an experienced neurologist or neurosurgeon should be capable of distinguishing between different kinds of strokes simply on clinical grounds. Strokes that are caused by an occlusion of a brain artery are usually ushered in with a sudden onset of a neurologic deficit, such as the loss of speech or unilateral paralysis. Such strokes tend to occur in older, hypertensive, or diabetic patients, who usually remain alert, have little or no headaches, and have no or only minimal clouding of consciousness. By contrast, hemorrhagic strokes, which also affect elderly, hypertensive, and diabetic patients, caused by a sudden spontaneous hemorrhage into the brain substance, are usually associated with severe headaches and a rapid onset of clouding or even the loss of consciousness. As for establishing the anatomic site of a lesion based on the neurologic examination, a versatile command of neuroanatomy and neurophysiology is necessary in order to correctly interpret the neurological findings as they relate to cerebral or spinal localization.

In order to place these thoughts into a clinical perspective, I should describe the case history of a patient who came to see Dr. Bucy in a second-opinion consultation after the patient was diagnosed with multiple sclerosis. This middle-aged accountant, confined to a wheel chair, displayed a multitude of neurologic symptoms. The initial symptom was slurred speech. This was followed by difficulty swallowing (even his own saliva), because of which he had several bouts with pneumonia. Lastly, he went on to develop a progressive paralysis of all four extremities. Such an unrelenting progression of symptoms was more consonant with a tumor rather than with multiple sclerosis, which tends to have a more undulating course, with periods of progression alternating with remissions. But where in relationship to the brain would this tumor be situated? Well, the neurological examination revealed that in addition to the numerous other deficits, the patient also had a weakness and atrophy of the left side of his tongue. Connecting the dots, Dr. Bucy surmised that this patient's illness began with a weakness and wasting of the left side of his tongue, which in turn caused the initial symptom of slurred speech. Since the paired twelfth cranial nerves initiate movements of the corresponding sides of the tongue, Dr. Bucy concluded that the anatomic location of the presumed tumor was in or around the lower brain stem, the medulla oblongata, in the vicinity of the origin of the left twelfth cranial nerve. As for any imaging studies, this patient was seen long before the CT, let alone the MRI era, and a cerebral angiogram was inconclusive. Dr. Bucy told the patient that the history of his illness suggested a tumor, potentially benign, rather than multiple sclerosis and that the neurological examination pointed to the lower brain stem as the site of the lesion. Dr. Bucy suggested to the patient they should proceed with surgery, based on the history and the neurological examination. This would be a technically difficult procedure even by today's standards, let alone in the early 1960s, considering the absence of technologies available today, such as the precise MRI-based image guidance technology, the operating microscope, and the intraoperative electrophysiological monitoring.

After being anesthetized, the patient was placed in a sitting upright position, popular among neurosurgeons at the time, with care being taken to maintain vital signs and prevent a potentially fatal pulmonary embolism should air enter the vascular pathways to the lungs through an open vein. Dr. Bucy proceeded to open the skull just above the nape through a vertical midline incision and a midline craniotomy. Fitted with a headlight, like a miner, he then opened the dura, which Dr. Bucy used to describe to his students as the inner "wallpaper" of the skull. The tumor became immediately visible underneath the second layer of tissue that envelopes the brain, the translucent arachnoid membrane.

No matter how many times they might have seen it, neurosurgeons cannot help but admire the wondrous splendor and the complexity of the anatomy revealed. There, in front of our eyes, bathed in glittering spinal fluid, was the slender ivory-colored brain stem—the seat of our consciousness and the conveyor of motor and sensory neural pathways—severely compressed and distorted by a reddish, walnut-sized benign nerve sheath tumor. A cascade of fragile cranial nerves emanating from the brain stem, some of which make our heart beat and others of which allow for the complex swallowing mechanism, and a leash of tortuous, pulsing arteries meandered around the tumor. One wrong move, injury to any one of these structures, be it neural or vascular, would have left the patient either unconscious; severely disabled; incapable of a meaningful, independent life; or dead. Determined and armed with a solid surgical plan and honed neurosurgical skills through years of experience, but not without fear out of the greatest respect for life with dignity, Dr. Bucy calmly began to reduce the tumor size by coring out the soft tumor interior. As the decompressed tumor capsule shrank, it receded from the brain stem and from the stretched cranial nerves and arteries. This made it possible to see behind the tumor, gently free it, and remove it completely without injury to the surrounding vital structures. The histological examination confirmed a benign (i.e., not cancerous) neuroma of the twelfth cranial nerve. With the tumor removed, Dr. Bucy asked me to close the wound, emphasizing the importance of this phase of the procedure, for even the smallest accumulation of blood can cause harm by compressing the brain stem once the skull is closed and reconstructed back to its original closed-box state. Referring to the closure part of the operation, Dr. Bucy used to say, "You have to pay just as much attention to landing a plane as to flying it."

The patient made a complete recovery with full restoration of neurological functions, except for a mild residual lisp in his speech. Witnessing Dr. Bucy's uncompromising respect for life with dignity as it relates to the preservation of neurologic functions and the richness of fundamentals learned from this and subsequent clinical evaluations and operative procedures at the hands of a master surgeon proved invaluable for my future life as a neurosurgeon.

FELLOWSHIPS IN NEW YORK AND MONTREAL

Dr. Bucy considered it important that his disciples be discerning in the microscopic anatomy of brain and spinal cord lesions. Hence, he arranged for me to spend six months with Dr. Harry Zimmerman, a noted neuropathologist at the Montefiore Hospital and the Mount Sinai Medical School in New York City. It was brutally cold in Chicago on that last day of December 1966, when I gathered my family and packed our cumulative belongings into our newly acquired and mirror-shine-polished navy-blue Chevrolet Malibu station wagon for the trip to New York City. We settled into our rented apartment on Rochambeau Avenue in the Bronx. New Year's Day was sparklingly sunny, ideal for sightseeing in the city. As we returned to the apartment, I discovered that our car had been broken into. The tires had been slashed, and the hood was covered with Scotch tape, defiling my oh-so-dearly and with-utmost-pride-applied polish. As I removed the tape, off came not only the polish but also the paint. Welcome to the Bronx!

Even though the time spent in Dr. Zimmerman's laboratory was valuable and intellectually stimulating, six months of neuropathology seemed an awfully long time when there was so much more to be learned in operative neurosurgery. Before embarking on the fellowship trip to New York, I was offered the position of an associate to Dr. Joseph Tarkington at the Evanston Hospital, a Northwestern teaching institution, which I accepted. By joining Dr. Tarkington in practice, I was assured of an academic appointment at Northwestern, which would give me the opportunity to work with and mentor neurosurgery residents. The appeal of working and living on Chicago's North Shore, with its lovely tree-lined suburbs, contributed to the decision.

During our discussions about my appointment to the staff as his associate, Dr. Tarkington suggested I also spend time with a friend from his residency days in Montreal, Dr. Claude Bertrand, one of the pioneers in the field of the surgical treatment of Parkinson's disease. Therefore, after an abbreviated fellowship in neuropathology, it was off again, hitting the road to Montreal. This was the time of the Montreal Expo, and the city was humming and bustling. My tenure at the Notre Dame Hospital was somewhat hampered by my not speaking French. Fortunately, I had only a few hands-on working exposures with the French Canadian patients. On the other hand, the neurosurgeons were all bilingual. Besides acquiring knowledge as to the pathophysiology of Parkinson's disease as it was understood at the time and learning the surgical technique of alleviating Parkinson's tremor from Dr. Bertrand, while at Notre Dame, I was also exposed to a novel surgical technique in the treatment of pituitary tumors. Dr. Bertrand's associate, Dr. Jules Hardy, a vibrant and perspicacious man brimming with new ideas and a master surgeon, introduced this technique. The novelty was the use of the operating microscope in conjunction with the transnasal approach to pituitary tumors. The transnasal technique was originally introduced at the turn of the twentieth century, only to be subsequently abandoned because of the rather confined and poorly illuminated operative field. It was not until Dr. Hardy introduced the operating microscope to the transnasal approach to the pituitary gland that this procedure was revived. To the best of my knowledge, upon joining the Evanston Hospital staff, I performed the first microscopic transnasal approach in the United States using Dr. Hardy's technique (known as the transsphenoidal operation) in November of 1967. As it turned out, the surgical treatment of pituitary tumors became the focus of my neurosurgical practice and of my academic endeavors.

GETTING STARTED

Dr. Joseph Tarkington was a plainspoken, straitlaced man who was completely unpretentious. To say that he was outspoken would be like saying that grass is green. He was also a charming and honest man and a terrific surgeon. While he did not go to any length to publish his results, Joe was locally known and respected for his enviable experience with arteriovenous malformations at a time when vascular neurosurgery was still in its infancy. When I interviewed for the job, the first thing he said was "Ciric, let us not do with four hands what two hands can do."

I have so many anecdotes about Joe that it would take all day to relate them, such as the time he said to me, "Hey, I can replace you with a five-cent postage stamp, but not her," pointing to his loyal scrub nurse. Also, while discussing an upcoming surgery with a patient, he was once overheard saying, "Green light, we proceed; red light, we stop. Any other questions?" Oh well, so much for informed consent. I will always remain grateful to Joe for taking me under his wing and for his lifelong friendship and mentorship.

To say that perceptions and attitudes as they relate to

neurosurgery have changed since I joined the Evanston Hospital staff in July of 1967 would be the understatement of the year. At that time, neurosurgery, while well established, was nevertheless a specialty in evolution, and the results were not always stellar. My first day on the job, I was asked by the chief of anesthesia, a taciturn former marine, "Ciric, do you know the difference between a neurosurgeon and a Mack truck?" Demurely, I responded, "No, sir, I do not," upon which he said without batting an eyelash, "Well, son, people occasionally survive being hit by a Mack truck." *Hmm*, I thought. *There is room for improvement.*

Thus, I settled into my professional life, committed to doing my best. As a graduate of the Northwestern residency program under the legendary Paul Bucy and having learned during my fellowship in Montreal the transnasal surgery for pituitary tumors using the surgical microscope, a novelty in neurosurgery in those times, I thought I knew everything there was to know about my specialty. I thought I was invincible and really a big shot. My delusions of grandeur were soon deflated, when a general practitioner from Highwood, a sardonic old-timer of Italian ancestry, called out from behind me as I was entering the hospital "Eh, boy, are you Joe's new sidekick?" It also did not help nurture my ego when a North Shore matron, after being examined by me at the office, said, "Dr. Ciric, you are such a kind doctor, and I want to thank you so much for diagnosing my problem. By the way, would you know of a good neurosurgeon to do the operation?" To add insult to injury, an elderly and somewhat-feckless internist at the Evanston Hospital approached me a few weeks later and, after taking off his spectacles, peered closely at the name on my lab coat and exclaimed,

"Ciric! Ciric, where did you get this funny name? Are you the guy who does hernias in Waukegan on the side?" At first, I did not understand what he meant. After all, I was a neurosurgeon who did not operate on hernias, and besides, I had never heard of Waukegan. Only later did I realize that this was when the American College of Surgeons, under Dr. Loyal Davis's leadership, battled the fee-splitting practice, and I suppose that is what "doing hernias in Waukegan on the side" meant. Be that as it may, the remark stung—as it was intended to.

Compared to today, these were also times when due process was much simpler. After one of my vituperative outbursts in the intensive care unit, when I was trying in vain to get the attention of nurses as I attended to a critically ill patient, I was called to the office of Dr. John Dorsey, a gaunt and elegant-to-a-T chief of surgery. Dr. Dorsey let me stand before him without offering me a seat. "I heard of your transgression," he said. "You don't really want me to transfer your file from the right bottom drawer of my desk, where I store the files of surgeons I keep, into the bottom drawer on the left side, where I toss the files of surgeons I let go." You can guess my answer.

While practicing neurosurgery in a teaching hospital like the Evanston Hospital met the standards of an aspiring academic neurosurgeon, providing neurosurgical care in a community hospital was not easy. To illustrate this, allow me to describe briefly my first operation in practice. Approximately two weeks after joining the staffs at the Evanston and several community hospitals, eager to start operating, I received a call at two o'clock in the morning from one of the community hospitals' emergency rooms, saying they had admitted an unconscious eighty-one-year-old lady who was found lying on the floor by her family. She had no focal signs, and her pupils were equal. The only abnormality was a bruise to her right temple. In 1967, there were no noninvasive diagnostic studies, such as the CT scan, let alone the MRI. The community hospital did not have capabilities for an angiogram either. The skull x-rays were negative. The laboratory results showed a marginally low glucose level. As I pondered what to do, I remembered the adage that if there is a suspicion for a traumatic intracranial hemorrhage, the neurosurgeon should proceed with exploratory bur holes, which I did, only to find nothing abnormal. Within hours after the operation, the patient woke up bright-eyed and bushy-tailed. It turned out that she was a diabetic who overdosed on insulin and hence recovered from the glucose infusion given during surgery. What was interesting, though, is that the patient's general practitioner, a senior fellow, thought I was a genius, and I was as good as gold in his eyes forever afterward.

CHRISTMAS 1968

The dining room was set for a festive Christmas dinner. There were plenty of reasons for Christmas cheer. We were a happy young couple and proud parents of two wonderful toddler daughters, and Anne was expecting our third child the following May. Moreover, I had landed a coveted job as a neurosurgeon in one of the most prestigious Chicagoland hospitals, one that was academically aligned with Northwestern University, where I was appointed assistant professor. On hand for the dinner were Anne's childhood friend Alice and her husband, Robert Marcy. Since I was on call, one of the travails of being the junior partner, I abstained from libations, which I served to our guests. Anne was about to pull the turkey out of the oven, allowing the enticing waft of the roast to permeate our small apartment and heighten the anticipation of a delicious meal, when the phone on the kitchen counter cut mercilessly through the cozy warmth of the evening. On the phone was the emergency room physician. "We just admitted a seven-year-old boy," the physician said. "B was brought by paramedics, unconscious after he was struck by a car while riding his bicycle." The examination by the ER doctor reportedly revealed blood and debris around a jagged laceration of about two inches in diameter over the left side of the boy's head. I was also assured that the boy's vital signs were stable; that, most importantly, his airway was free; and that his respirations were unencumbered. In the absence of noninvasive diagnostic studies, I requested that a portable skull x-ray be obtained in the ER and simply added, "I am on my way." Taking leave from my guests and family, I urged them not to wait and told them to proceed with dinner in my absence. Thankfully, Anne has been the ideal neurosurgeon's wife—she never objected to my heeding the unpredictable calls to duty at a moment's notice over family obligations, something that had marred the marriages of some of my colleagues.

I ran down the stairs of our apartment building on Maple Street in Evanston and took Ridge Road to the hospital. This being Christmas, the traffic was light, and I sped along, hoping that the traffic cops would not be lurking around, waiting for speeders, until after people would be returning from dinner at a later hour.

I entered the ER somewhat apprehensive that the child's condition could have gotten worse over the time it took me to reach the hospital. I was relieved to find that the child was breathing freely and that his vital signs were still stable. On neurologic examination, B was unresponsive when I called him by his name or asked him to squeeze my fingers placed in the palms of his hands. He responded to a gentle pressure on the breastbone by withdrawing his arms appropriately in a defensive posture, albeit more vigorously with his left than his right arm. In a rudimentary way, this signified that the connection between B's brain and his brain stem and spinal cord was largely intact, with the caveat that the performance of the left side of his brain seemed to lag behind the robust response of the right one.

With a surgical mask covering my mouth and nose and with my hands scrubbed and gloved, I removed the dressing and examined the wound in the frontal area, about half an inch from the midline. In doing so, it became immediately clear that the debris described by the ER physician was in fact particulate brain tissue. This ominous finding along with a glance at the skull x-rays, which showed small bubbles of air inside the head, confirmed that the boy had sustained a compound depressed skull fracture. The remainder of the evaluation obtained prior to my arrival, including x-rays of the spine and routine laboratory tests, indicated that all was normal. In short, I was facing a depressed skull fracture with the broken skull fragments likely imbedded in the brain substance. I realized that the jagged margins of the depressed fragments could create more havoc by cutting into a brain artery, causing hemorrhaging and a clot to form inside the brain. The other danger was the possibility of meningitis, as dirt from the scalp could have been driven into the brain along with the skull fragments. In any event, there was also the possibility of permanent brain damage and of epileptic seizures in the long run. A compound depressed skull fracture, therefore, constitutes a neurosurgical emergency with only a short window of time available to avert a cascading series of complications. With this in mind, I alerted the operating room as to the pending emergency even before I talked to the family.

In the family waiting room, I met with B's distraught parents. I explained the nature of their son's brain injury and the rationale for emergency surgery. Compared to an elective surgical procedure, when the neurosurgeon's reputation precedes him, under emergency circumstances, when the family is facing the neurosurgeon for the first time and with no time to spare, it is more difficult to establish the necessary trust. In order to convey effectively the nature of the injury, treatment recommendation, and prognosis, the neurosurgeon has to communicate calmly, confidently, and with empathy, and he has to be cogent by using words that are easily understood by the family. The tenor of the surgeon's message must not be patronizing, let alone supercilious, and must instead be one of respect. He or she must patiently respond to the family's queries, no matter how immaterial they might sound, and always be truthful and steeped in hope but not promise. It is usually advantageous to have as many of the patient's family members present as possible, as the surgeon's message can be distorted through hearsay. Fortunately, B's parents understood the situation well and consented to surgery.

The surgical strategy was to expose the healthy tissues around the depressed fracture first and then proceed with the repair centripetally, from healthy tissues to the core of the injury. Attempting the opposite, by reaching immediately for the imbedded skull fragments, would be to risk a greater degree of brain laceration or cause a tear in a brain artery. With the patient anesthetized and appropriately positioned on the operating table, the hair was shaved about an inch wide around the laceration. The laceration itself was then cleansed using copious irrigation with sterile physiologic saline solution, and the surrounding skin was prepped and draped in the routine manner. By enlarging the star-shaped laceration, we exposed the surrounding normal-appearing skull for about half an inch. After placing a bur hole the size of a dime through the healthy skull, adjacent to the depressed fragments, we used a special bone-cutting instrument to remove approximately a third-of-an-inch rim of healthy skull circumferentially around the depressed fragments. This maneuver exposed the sheet covering the brain, the dura, surrounding the depressed skull fracture. With the overhead lights dimmed, the operating microscope was brought into position, enabling us to view the details of the injury magnified and brilliantly illuminated. The depressed skull fragments had penetrated into the brain and were held in place by the lacerated margins of the dura. There was a small blood clot surrounding the bone fragments. The jagged dura laceration was inadequate to visualize the brain behind the depressed bony fragments, making it impossible to estimate precisely the extent of brain injury itself without opening the dura further. Choosing the most appropriate site for it, the dura was opened about half an inch away from the lacerated dura margins, and the incision was extended toward the lacerated dura until the two openings were connected. The three bone fragments that were in a way strangulated by the torn dura relaxed and could now be extracted from the brain without difficulty. One of the depressed fragments was precariously adjacent to a brain artery that we could safely keep out of harm's way as we worked under the microscope. The brain laceration itself was then clearly visible and could be thoroughly cleaned of all debris. The dura was sutured shut using the tissue underneath the scalp as a graft to cover the gaps where the dura margins could not be approximated. As for closing the skull defect, we chose to replace the bony fragments, which in the meantime had been thoroughly cleaned and soaked in

IVAN CIRIC, MD

an antibiotic solution. With the bone fragments in place as if puzzle pieces and secured to the surrounding cranium, the operative site was thoroughly washed out with an antibiotic solution, the scalp was closed in layers, and a dressing was applied. By the time I met with the family in the waiting area, it was around midnight. The family was relieved after learning the good news that the operation had proceeded as planned and that their son was doing fine. The expression of gratitude by the family was a heartwarming experience. After assuring everyone that the patient was stable, I drove home, savoring the exhilarating feeling of a battle won. B did well over the years, with no untoward neurologic consequences.

While the diagnosis of an open head trauma, such as in the afore-described case, was relatively straightforward, a precise diagnosis as to the extent of a closed head injury prior to the availability of contemporary noninvasive imaging studies was challenging, to say the least. Shortly after I began practicing, I was called to the emergency room to attend to a lovely nineteen-year-old college student who, while on Easter break, sustained a head injury in a bicycle accident. She had a bruise over the left forehead, was lethargic, and exhibited signs of weakness in her left extremities. A bilateral cerebral angiogram was obtained, which showed evidence of a large blood clot overlying the right side of the brain, known as a subdural hematoma. Following the removal of the hematoma, she woke up from the anesthetic and was fully awake in the recovery room, only to become mentally clouded once again, lapsing rapidly into unconsciousness. A repeat angiogram showed a large *left* frontal epidural hematoma, for which she had to be rushed back to the operating room. I suspect that after the right subdural hematoma was removed, the initially small left epidural hematoma began to expand, as it became unopposed by the counterpressure from the right side. In retrospect, the unrecognized left epidural hematoma could have been discovered had the patient had an additional oblique view of the angiogram to better visualize the frontal area of the skull and brain. It took several weeks for this beautiful young woman to recover her basic neurological functions.

THE CONUNDRUM OF CEREBRAL ANEURYSMS

A cerebral aneurysm is a blister on a brain artery. An aneurysm is usually found at the point where an artery branches into two smaller arteries. The hypothesis is that at the branching of an artery, the three-layer thickness of the arterial wall is missing its sturdy muscular middle layer. Consequently, under the jet-stream pressure of the circulating blood, the vessel wall begins to pouch out as an aneurismal sac. Not all aneurysms burst, but many do. Since all intracranial arteries, before entering the brain, are inside the arachnoid membrane, which envelops the brain as a translucent sac, a ruptured aneurysm causes the blood to pour out into the subarachnoid space. The presence of blood in the subarachnoid space is known as subarachnoid hemorrhage. The hallmark symptom of a ruptured aneurysm is a sudden, violent headache, in conjunction with nausea, vomiting, and stiffness in the neck. In response to the presence of blood in the subarachnoid space, the arteries near a ruptured aneurysm constrict, or go into a spasm, in neurosurgical jargon. If the spasm is pronounced, it can lead to a lack of blood supply downstream from the aneurysm, resulting in a stroke-like clinical picture, including loss of consciousness, paralysis, and other neurological deficits, depending on the location of the aneurysm. The phenomenon of an arterial spasm secondary to a ruptured aneurysm has been the subject of much decades-long scientific scrutiny, with no uniform answer as to its cause and with no singularly effective treatment. In addition, the presence of blood in the subarachnoid space can hinder the normal brain fluid circulation, resulting in an accumulation of fluid under pressure inside the brain, a condition usually referred to as hydrocephalus, as I discussed earlier. Another ill effect of a subarachnoid hemorrhage is the formation of a blood clot inside the brain when the aneurysm ruptures in the immediate vicinity of the brain substance. Based on the patient's condition in the immediate aftermath of a ruptured aneurysm, a subarachnoid hemorrhage is classified into five grades of prognostic significance. Patients in good condition are classified as having grades I or II subarachnoid hemorrhage, with grades IV and V denoting severe neurologic impairment. The only effective treatment for a ruptured aneurysm is to exclude it from the circulation. This can be accomplished by performing a craniotomy and excluding the aneurysm from circulation by applying a V-shaped clip to the neck of the aneurismal pouch or, if this is not possible, by reinforcing the wall of the aneurismal sac. Conversely, the aneurysm can be occluded from within by filling the aneurysm sac with tiny (less than a hair in diameter) metallic coils using a series of catheters that are introduced into the circulation via an artery in the groin and threaded under x-ray control to the neck of the aneurysm. In time, other similar endovascular techniques have been devised. The dilemma as to how and when to proceed with the repair of an aneurysm, if at all, is the subject of an ongoing debate among aneurysm surgeons, especially for patients in whom a nonruptured aneurysm was discovered incidentally. The adjudication to that end must consider the location of the aneurysm, the stage of the aneurismal rupture, the patient's age and health, and, in a nonruptured aneurysm, the statistical likelihood of a rupture. The various options must be discussed thoroughly with the patient and family, so they can make a considered decision before consenting to the operation.

About a month after starting in practice, I was making rounds at the hospital one Sunday morning, when my beeper went off. The call came from the department of psychiatry. "A patient was found unconscious," said the psychiatry resident when I contacted her. "She is in room 5905." After the psychiatry resident assured me that the patient's airway was free and that she was breathing spontaneously, I rushed along with my resident, a fellow from Thailand on assignment to our hospital from the Northwestern residency program, to the patient's bedside on the fifth floor, taking two stairs at a time. The story I got was that the patient, a fifty-six-year-old teacher, was admitted to the psychiatry ward by a friend two days prior because she was "acting crazily" and was delirious, thrashing around, and complaining of severe headaches. Evidently, in the throes of one such bout with severe headaches, the patient suddenly gasped, moaned, and fell unconscious in her bed. The story was consistent with a subarachnoid hemorrhage secondary to a ruptured aneurysm. On examination, the patient was unresponsive to verbal stimuli and tended to stretch out both arms rather than to flex them in a defensive manner when slight pressure was applied to her breastbone. Such a response is a poor prognostic sign that indicates significant involvement of the brain stem.

The patient's pupils were equal, midsized, and they did not react to light. A cerebral angiogram was obtained within fifteen minutes. At that time, a cerebral angiography was performed by directly puncturing the carotid artery in the neck and injecting an iodine-based solution to outline the intracranial vessels in search of an aneurysm. The angiogram showed a small aneurysm, no greater than four millimeters, in the anterior cerebral artery circulation, pointing upward, toward the bottom of the cerebral cavity (the third ventricle). The intracranial vessels were in spasm and stretched, secondary to abnormal accumulations of brain fluid under pressure in the lateral ventricles. The hydrocephalus was caused by an extension of hemorrhage into the third ventricle blocking brain fluid from flowing out of the lateral ventricles. The prognosis for survival, let alone for any semblance of a quality life, was grave. In short, the patient had a grade IV to V subarachnoid hemorrhage. After reaching her only relative (a sister in Seattle) by phone, I explained the nature of the critical situation at hand, the treatment options, and the poor prognosis. In spite of the poor prognosis, the sister asked me to proceed with surgery.

After inserting a temporary tube into the patient's lateral ventricle to relieve the accumulated brain fluid, we proceeded with the craniotomy to expose the ruptured aneurysm. The aneurysm was difficult to locate due to a limited exposure underneath the swollen brain and due to the surrounding hemorrhage. Postoperatively, the patient did poorly and passed away within twenty-four hours after surgery. The defeat was complete. Even though the prognosis was dismal, the misery of failing was a new and crushing experience that I never quite learned to cope with as a practicing neurosurgeon over the ensuing five decades. Nothing prepared me during my residency for a situation like this, where the patient succumbs after a personal futile effort. To be sure, during my residency, I witnessed many intra- and postoperative failures, but these unfortunate happenings were always at the hands of and under the ultimate responsibility of the senior man, such as the department chair or the attending neurosurgeon. To call the nearest of kin and say that the loved one had passed away was also a novel emotional experience that I had to approach with utmost professionalism, truthfully and compassionately. What could I have done differently to change the outcome? Probably little, if anything at all, for the prognosis of a grade V aneurismal rupture was dismal to begin with. Nevertheless, this unfortunate outcome made me decide to use the operating microscope in each of my subsequent operations on cerebral aneurysms. My decision was reinforced by the published reports in the neurosurgical literature that extolled the benefits of the operating microscope. I also traveled abroad so I could observe firsthand the virtuosity of Professor Gazi Yasargil in Zurich, Switzerland, and Dr. Charles Drake in Ontario, Canada, as they performed operations on cerebral aneurysms using the operating microscope and microsurgical techniques.

LIFE OR DEATH, NEUROLOGIC INTEGRITY OR LIFELONG DISABILITY

I was called to the emergency department on an otherwise-lazy summer afternoon to see a forty-five-year-old woman with an acute, sudden, bursting headache. S was fully alert and neurologically intact. On examination, the only abnormal finding was stiffness in her neck. The CT scan confirmed the presence of a subarachnoid hemorrhage. The cerebral angiogram showed a three-millimeter aneurysm on her right carotid artery, less than half an inch after it enters the skull, at the point where a small vessel, known by the acronym of PCOM, branches off. By the time the angiogram was done, it was already late in the evening. After discussing the clinical and angiogram findings with the patient and her husband, I also explained the available treatment options, all with the aim of preventing the aneurysm from rupturing again, possibly with a lethal outcome. I recommended proceeding with craniotomy to occlude the aneurysm as the most effective method of preventing a recurrent hemorrhage. In my opinion, the benefits of surgery outweighed the risks, which I explained in detail. I suggested that we proceed with surgery early the following morning in order to have the optimal operating conditions—as opposed to starting the operation at midnight. The patient and her husband were agreeable with this decision. I went home to catch up with some sleep. As I lay in bed, going through the steps of the operation, my thoughts blended imperceptibly into dreams of the operation.

As I entered the room in the holding area early the following morning, I greeted S with a smile on my face and an apprehension in my soul I have always experienced when facing surgery for aneurysm repairs in patients with grade I or II subarachnoid hemorrhages. In contrast to patients with grades IV to V subarachnoid hemorrhages whose dismal prognosis for recovery following surgery is largely dependent on their poor preoperative neurologic condition, the prognosis in patients with grades I to II subarachnoid hemorrhages, who are in good condition, is additionally influenced by the neurosurgeon's skill and experience. I was fully aware, therefore, that the outcome of the operation, life or death, neurologic integrity or lifelong disability, rested in my hands. The only way to honestly accept and reciprocate the patient's trust in me was by way of a salutary outcome. My uneasiness got a boost when S said to me, "Doctor Ciric, I feel so much better this morning. Do we really need to do this, with all the risks you explained to us?" I took her hand in mine and said that the reason she felt better was that the three doses of an anti-inflammatory steroid she had received overnight had kicked in, reducing the irritation the hemorrhage had caused surrounding her brain. I also added that the danger of another bleed was not only the same but would increase with the passage of time as the clot covering the point of rupture gradually dissolved, opening once again the flood gate for a recurrent hemorrhage.

After being anesthetized, S was positioned supine on the operating table, with her head turned some twenty degrees toward the left and slightly inclined toward the floor to provide a good line of vision toward the base of the brain. A skin incision reminiscent of a question mark, starting from about two inches above the middle of the right eyebrow and ending just in front of the right ear, was made by the neurosurgery resident with me assisting. The skull was entered via a craniotomy at the junction of the right temple and the frontal bone. However, in order to gain sufficient maneuvering room to occlude the aneurysm, which was tucked deeply under the brain, a part of the skull base had to be drilled away as well.

Let me stop here for a moment to mention that I have often thought of the sequential connotations of a neurosurgical procedure. It all starts with the momentary ethical trepidation the instant before the scalpel first penetrates the skin of another human being, no matter how lofty the reason behind it. This short-lived uneasiness merges imperceptibly into the craft-like routine of opening the head. In the next phase of vanquishing the specific pathology, the operation becomes an intuitive art, only to blend again into craft during the closure of the wound. The circle closes once again with the ethics of assessing one's performance honestly and truthfully after surgery, when meeting the family in the waiting area.

Switching seats with the neurosurgery resident, I asked that the microscope be brought into position. Working comfortably under the microscope, I opened the dura and the arachnoid membranes that envelop the brain. This exposed the corridor between the frontal and temporal lobes. By separating the two lobes gently, I came upon the major branch of the carotid artery, known by the acronym of MCA. Following the path of this red river of life down to its origin brought the carotid artery and the aneurysm into view. This proceeded slowly, as there was a small blood clot enveloping the carotid artery and the aneurysm. Any rash move could have displaced the scab covering the opening in the aneurysm, leading to a brisk hemorrhage that would have instantly obscured the field—a frightening occurrence dreaded by every aneurysm surgeon. After gently flushing out the clot, I could see under a high-power microscope magnification the swirling of blood behind the thin aneurysm wall. Neurosurgeons have at their disposal a whole assortment of different-sized and variously shaped aneurysm clips. I chose a curved clip of appropriate size that I could apply to the base of the aneurysm without encroaching on the carotid artery itself. Placing the clip on an aneurysm is the zenith of the operation. There is no question that being calm, cool, and collected and having a steady hand are the prerequisites for a successful clip application. Yet at that moment, deep down on a visceral level, neurosurgeons feel something akin to a shiver running down their spines. The effervescent, physically and emotionally pleasing sense of relief that neurosurgeons experience after a successful clipping of an aneurysm is beyond description.

As she woke up from the anesthetic in the recovery room, S's first questions were "Are we done? Can I go home now?" I was on cloud nine. I nearly hopscotched my way to the family waiting area to bring the good news to her husband and children. Oh, how wonderful it felt to be hugged! I reciprocated in kind and from the heart. S remained a lifelong grateful patient.

SPRUCE STREET

The initial wages for a neurosurgeon in 1967 were conspicuously inadequate for the purchase of a home in the heart of Chicago's northern suburbs, where public schools offer a scholarly atmosphere and an environment conducive to creativity. So for a couple of years, we rented an apartment in Evanston. Eventually, we were able to put a down payment on our first home at Spruce and Hibbard Road in Winnetka, which we furnished with eclectic pieces, including French antiques collected by Anne as a hobby while still single and the restored Biedermeier furniture from my aunt's cellar. We also added a glass-enclosed, winterized patio to the living room. This was a neat two-story, three-bedroom clapboard house with a beautiful light-colored wood-paneled den and library. As for the yard, I frequently tell the story of how our neighbor reminded me one day that the unencumbered growth of grass needed attention. To that end, he suggested I rent a cow. Well, I got the message—and a lawn mower. Alas, the trouble was that being a compulsive, obsessive neurosurgeon, I was never satisfied with the evenness of the mowed lawn, necessitating another and another attempt at mowing, until the barren earth showed underneath my masterly effort at landscaping, much to Anne's chagrin and my neighbor's benevolent delight.

Living on Spruce Street was just right for a young professional and his family. Shortly before we moved to Spruce Street, our son was born. He was a shy little boy who loved his stuffed animals and deferred to his older sisters, who, by virtue of their seniority, called shots. When he was two months old, we woke him up on July 20, 1969, so he could one day say that he witnessed the incredible feat of humankind, the first man on the moon. In the perhaps-mistaken belief that boys should be playing ice hockey, I enrolled my son in the Winnetka Park District peewee hockey program, with me as a lowly assistant coach. He became a superb skater, although I am not sure his heart was in the rough-and-tumble sport of hockey. Be that as it may, the following year, the Winnetka Mites won the Illinois State Championship. My son's interest in hockey in the wake of this win gradually waned.

Spruce Street was also where Anne's mother and my mother used to visit from Europe. We always vacationed with our children as a family, even taking our kids to professional conferences. Summer vacations were spent in Eagle River in northern Wisconsin. We also ventured out west to Colorado, driving in our Ford station wagon with no air-conditioning—a remarkable feat, especially upon reaching the arid planes of North Platte in Nebraska at the end of July. In time, we traded our Ford for a Buick Estate Wagon with air-conditioning, which I drove to work well into my preretirement years. The unusually long tenure of my Estate Wagon did not go unnoticed by a colleague orthopedic surgeon and new-car aficionado, who repeatedly bugged me to get a new car. One day, out of sheer frustration, I responded to his haranguing by saying, "David, I just bought a new car." His eyes lit up in anticipation when he asked, "What did you get?" to which I responded in jest and with ultimate nonchalance, "A secondhand Yugo." How disgusted this sophisticated car buff would have been had he seen the oh-so-plebeian plastic covers I purchased to protect the wagon's seats from being soiled by my kids. The Estate Wagon was also a matter of gossip among the nurses, some of whom suggested I hang little curtains on the side windows and sleep in it, since my profession necessitated that I stay in the hospital till the wee hours—or were they trying to imply something else?

The ten years we lived on Spruce Street were professionally challenging, as I was building my brain tumor, pituitary, and skull-base surgery practice at the Evanston Hospital while at the same time endeavoring to improve the neurosurgical service at the Highland Park Hospital, all of which required frequent shuttling between the two institutions, a distance of approximately fifteen miles. Besides my clinical practice, my academic activities—including teaching Northwestern neurosurgery residents on rotation at the Evanston Hospital, preparing presentations at national meetings, and writing and publishing—took up many of my waking hours. Looking back, I can see that anxieties induced by such a hectic schedule contributed to my occasional highly volatile reactions to innocent disagreements with Anne or our children on minor family matters. Upon coming home, no matter how late, I would ward off my frustrations by jogging regularly, weather permitting. Fortunately, these frustrations subsided as my practice matured with a growing reputation and increased peer recognition for my clinical and academic endeavors.

THE CURSE OF PRIMARY BRAIN TUMORS

Neurosurgeons generally enjoy the wide range of surgical interventions in their purview, from a nearly countless array of spinal procedures to a kaleidoscopic variety of cranial operations, from removal of brain tumors and repair of vascular lesions, such as cerebral aneurysms, to pediatric and functional neurosurgery. At the same time, such a diversity of neurosurgical procedures might also be a hindrance to mastering the entire repertoire of procedures to perfection. To my thinking, in neurosurgery, the adage of being the jack-of-all-trades does not necessarily ring wise, so in keeping with my proclivities, in time, I decided to shift my focus toward the operative treatment of intracranial tumors and spinal surgery and away from the vascular, pediatric, functional, and other subspecialty neurosurgical procedures. I had the luxury of doing so, as over time, I had surrounded myself with a team of experts across the spectrum of neurosurgery to whom I could refer a ruptured cerebral aneurysm or a pediatric patient who came my way while I was on emergency duty.

In keeping with my neurosurgical upbringing under Paul Bucy, I maintained a career-long interest in the surgical treatment of primary brain tumors. Primary brain tumors originate from the brain structure's supportive cell lines, the brain matrix, and not from the precious neurons. The majority of primary brain tumors are, unfortunately, malignant in nature. Neuropathologists classify these tumors in four grades according to the degree of malignancy. The highest grade is the dreaded glioblastoma multiforme, or glioblastoma for short. Glioblastoma strikes mercilessly regardless of age or gender, although middle-aged individuals are the predominant victims. The central core of a glioblastoma, consisting of pure virulent tumor tissue, is bordered by an area where the tumor cells have infiltrated imperceptibly into the surrounding normal brain. The microscopic examination of the core of a glioblastoma typically shows numerous malformed glia cells that rapidly replicate into new malignant cells. As the rapid tumor growth outpaces the sprouting of new arterial vessels in a futile effort to supply the tumor with oxygen and nutrients, parts of the tumor undergo decay. The tumor causes swelling of the surrounding brain, resulting in symptoms of increased intracranial pressure. In accordance with Dr. Bucy's seminal report on the surgical treatment of malignant brain tumors, the majority of neurosurgeons worldwide have adopted the adage of a "gross total removal" of the central core of the tumor that no longer resembles normal brain as the gospel for alleviating the patient's symptoms and prolonging life. Following the surgical removal of the core of the tumor, the surrounding more-normal-appearing brain tissue, which nevertheless contains malignant tumor cells, is then treated with radiation and chemotherapies. The science and art of the surgical strategy involve recognizing the acceptable limits of a resection—how much of the surrounding brain tissue, which has been infiltrated by the tumor but is otherwise functioning, can also be removed in order to achieve the maximum short- and long-term benefits while still safeguarding brain functions? The neurosurgeon has more latitude in this regard in the noneloquent areas and is considerably restricted in the eloquent areas of the brain, such as the movement or vision centers or close to the cognitive, memory, and speech centers. Meanwhile, progress has been made with the introduction of ever-more-sophisticated techniques of intraoperative demonstration of tumor margins and of methods designed to preserve the surrounding eloquent brain tissue. These include the intravenous injection of fluorescent or other dyes, which penetrate into the tumor tissue and are recognizable under the microscope. In addition, electrophysiological monitoring of brain functions, with the patient either anesthetized or only sedated in order to be able to communicate with the patient during the procedure, has also become an essential part of a complex brain operation, especially when carried out in the vicinity of cognitive and speech centers.

Besides the usual evaluation of the patient's medical condition, one of the important steps leading up to the surgery is the preoperative discussion with the patient and family. By virtue of their training, during which they have witnessed numerous similar encounters at the sides of their mentors, neurosurgeons are well equipped to convey a truthful, credible, and compassionate message that contains at least a ray of hope, for hope is at the core of human life. During their training and later on in their professional lives, neurosurgeons are exposed to a wide variety of neurologic illnesses and injuries, often ones that are life threatening and, more frequently, threatening to imperil the essential brain functions. The multitude of these experiences allows neurosurgeons to accrue a completely new spectrum of sensitivity nuances that they can avail themselves of, since each new patient or family requires a highly personalized dialogue. Such individualized interaction between the surgeon and the brain tumor patient establishes the necessary trust and remains the cornerstone of the physician-patient relationship for the duration of a patient's life. This trust facilitates not only the discussion regarding the necessity for surgery versus alternative but less-efficacious treatment options but also the discussion about the short-term outlook, including the potential for operative and postoperative complications, and the long-term prognosis. My approach to that end was to explain the nature and the location of the tumor with the aid of available images, relate the sequence of the operative steps with the help of a skull and brain model when appropriate, and patiently answer all questions. Over the years, I have become utterly convinced that patients appreciate being on the receiving end of unhurried visits during which they are treated with deepest respect for their needs and sensitivities so that their fears are best alleviated when they understand the ramifications of surgery. There is no substitute for taking the time to cogently and congenially level with the patient and family during preoperative discussions. When a surgeon does so, the patient and family, regardless of the level of their education, are more likely to comprehend and accept the surgical indications, the basic tenets and technical details of the operation itself, and the expected outcome, including the surgical risks. As always, there are exceptions to such a deliberate acquiescence of the notion of a pending cranial surgery. There are always a few patients, though, who are generally mistrustful and who never exhibit the necessary level of comfort and confidence, no matter how many opinions they have solicited. There might also be a relative who, having missed the exhaustive preoperative discussions or for a different reason (not infrequently out of feelings of personal guilt), displays a lack of trust at best and engages in acrimonious recriminations at worst. To deal with such family members requires even more patience and goodwill in order to lessen their anger and put them on the same page with other family members.

Neurosurgeons have different ways of preparing themselves for the actual operative procedures. I personally preferred a quiet evening at home, going over the details of the upcoming surgery, because an anticipatory analysis of the operative and postoperative ramifications of an operation is essential to prevent complications. Indeed, in neurosurgery more than in any other specialty, a compulsive attention to detail during the entire cascade of events, from the preoperative preparation to the day of discharge from the hospital, is the key to a successful surgical endeavor. Each neurosurgeon develops a personal set of bedside manners based on his or her upbringing, proclivities, and social astuteness. On the morning of surgery, I used to visit with the patient and family along with my resident and a nurse in the preoperative holding area in order to put the patient at ease through a genuinely upbeat conversation during which I would again remind the patient of the salient surgical indications and of the expected outcome. I also touched upon potential operative and postoperative side effects and complications, previously discussed with the patient on an outpatient basis, without going into repetitive and exhausting details. Indeed, obtaining an informed consent is an art that requires a balanced approach to truth and hope.

As for the preoperative imaging of patients with brain

tumors, over the past thirty years, there have been extraordinary developments in the diagnostic armamentarium. The magnetic resonance imaging (MRI) has been the mainstay of brain tumor imaging. The last decade has also brought further refinement in MRI technology in terms of the functional MRI, which is capable of discerning eloquent areas of the brain, such as the motor and sensory speech areas, the visual cortex, and the like. Besides identifying the eloquent cortical functions, an even-more-novel MRI-based technology, known as diffusion tensor imaging (DTI), has made it possible to trace neural pathways in the depth of the brain. This has proven of particular value when operating on deep-seated tumors, because it enables neurosurgeons to skirt around critical neural pathways deeper into the brain.

Up to a certain point, the operation itself is a sequence of well-established steps that require utmost attention to detail. To begin with, the anesthetized patient has to be positioned on the operating table for a lengthy procedure in such a manner that the patient's eyes and the dependent body parts are protected from undue pressure. As for the sterile preparation and draping of the operative field, the established techniques have changed over the years in accordance with data-driven evidence. For example, presently, the head is not shaved, except for a trough of hair approximating the intended incision line. The process of opening the skull vault, the craniotomy itself, is also a well-established sequence of operating maneuvers, albeit not without risks, which are not always heralded enough during the preoperative discussions though are certainly heeded by all experienced neurosurgeons. One such complication comes to mind. During a craniotomy in the vicinity of large venous channels contained within the inner wallpaper of the skull (the dura), a venous channel can be breeched, resulting in a torrential and, at times, lethal hemorrhage. The tear in the channel can also become the point of entry of ambient air into the circulation, causing a potentially fatal air embolism. Such a catastrophic event is more likely to occur if the patient's head is positioned above the level of the heart, in which case the air can enter the bloodstream rapidly due to the atmospheric pressure being greater than the intravascular pressure in the channel. To ward off tedium and in order to get into the rhythm of an operation, a good number of my colleagues listen to music during surgery. Personally, I never subscribed to that custom, since I believe that it distracts from concentration. "Have you ever seen Tiger Woods tee off while listening to music?" has been my preferred reply when asked about music in the operating room.

At the beginning of my neurosurgical career, the approach to an intrinsic malignant brain tumor was based principally on the neurosurgeon's three-dimensional subjective perception of the two-dimensional imaging studies. Metaphorically speaking, this would be like attempting to estimate the location of a smaller ball within a larger ball and figuring out how to reach for it without veering off target—certainly a daunting task requiring a great deal of intuition based on experience honed through repetition and time, not to mention an intimate knowledge of neuroanatomy. It is not surprising that while operating in the depth of the brain, even the most experienced neurosurgeon of yesteryear would occasionally miss the mark. In order to correct the trajectory to the tumor, the neurosurgeon would then be compelled to mark the location in the brain with a radiopaque marker, close the operative site, and take the anesthetized patient back to the radiology suite for an imaging study to identify the relationship between the temporary marker and the brain tumor position. In the last decade, there has been remarkable progress, however, in MRI-based intracranial navigation technology, to a point where neurosurgeons can reach for and operate on deep-seated tumors through minimally invasive surface ports and least-injurious corridors through the brain with utmost precision.

The removal of a deep-seated malignant brain tumor that does not reveal itself on the surface requires a surgeon to make an incision into the cerebral cortex and open a corridor through the underlying white matter, preferably choosing the shortest route to the tumor and using the groove (sulcus) between two adjacent cortical hillocks (gyrus) as the point of entry. Yet under certain circumstances, it is necessary to choose an alternate and more circuitous route in order to avoid breeching the eloquent subcortical white matter tracts. Once the tumor has been accessed, the preferred removal technique is to follow the demonstrable tumor margins circumferentially until it is freed from the surrounding white matter.

Over the past decades, the mechanics of tumor removal have also become safer, not only through the use of the operating microscope and, more recently, of the endoscopic techniques but also through the employment of a variety of novel tumor removal technologies, such as the ultrasound-based surgical technique that breaks down and aspirates the tumor tissue. All along, a thorough hemostasis is necessary to keep the operative field bloodless at all times. In the process of tumor removal, neurosurgeons must also safeguard essential arterial and venous channels, because an occlusion of a critically important blood vessel can result in a stroke. In fact, vascular injuries account for a significant number of the postoperative neurologic complications.

In spite of this progress in diagnostic tools and surgical technology, there has not been a substantial commensurate breakthrough in terms of the survival of a patient harboring a glioblastoma. The same can be said for the remarkable advances in radiation oncology and chemotherapy designed to either thwart the replication of malignant cells or to deprive them of blood supply and, thus, nourishment. When I began my residency in 1963, the average survival time for a glioblastoma was nine months. Today, more than fifty years later, the average survival time is twelve to fourteen months. The main reason for this is that although glioblastomas might look alike under the pathologist's microscope, they are all different in their molecular biology, invalidating the one-treatment-fits-all tumors precept. This is why individualized immunotherapy, based on creating antibodies to a specific tumor antigen, appears to be a more promising treatment. As for the prognosis, younger patients in whom the tumor is localized in the noneloquent areas of the brain, such as the frontal or temporal lobes of the nondominant hemisphere, and far enough from the speech, motor, or sensory centers usually fair better than the stated survival average. A salutary postoperative quality of life and the duration of survival also depend on the extent of tumor removal—the more the better. Every so often, the glioblastoma will randomly strike a prominent individual, bringing the curse of these vicious tumors and the plight of those who suffer from them to public awareness. Clearly, more research supported by governmental and private industry grants is very much needed.

Primary brain tumors of a lesser grade retain some of the characteristics of the cellular line they originate from, hence the various tongue-twisting names for these tumors, such as astrocytomas, oligodendrogliomas, and the like. Astrocytomas originate from astrocytes, the most numerous of the brain matrix supportive cells. Similarly, oligodendrogliomas derive from oligodendroglia, another brain matrix supportive cell line. Lower-grade primary brain tumors are frequently accompanied by epileptic seizures or, due to their slow growth, a gradual progression of neurologic symptoms, such as the loss of strength or coordination. In contrast to glioblastomas, whose MRI images show tumor enhancement—metaphorically speaking, they blush up upon the injection of a ferromagnetic contrast material due to a breakdown in the blood-brain barrier—there is no such enhancement in the MRI images of lower-grade primary brain tumors. Nevertheless, this imaging difference is not reliable-enough information to definitively establish the degree of a tumor's malignancy. Consequently, in order to arrive at a correct diagnosis, one must obtain a tissue sample for detailed examination by the neuropathologist. A tissue sample can be obtained either by performing a biopsy—a rather low-risk procedure, performed under local anesthesia, that utilizes MRI-based navigation technology—or by removing the tumor via a formal craniotomy, as described earlier. The decision on which way to proceed depends on the geography of the tumor. A good number of lower-grade primary brain tumors infiltrate diffusely through a large territory deep in the brain, in the region of the deep-seated gray matter, known as the basal ganglia, which are indispensable for human life and function. They can also envelop the deep motor fiber tracts and surround the arterial blood vessels traversing the brain. If those structures were injured or surgically shut off, the result would be a permanently disabling stroke. The inability to surgically remove some of these tumors is not necessarily synonymous with a battle lost. Tissue samples obtained via biopsies might reveal important information as to the precise nature of tumors, some of which are eminently sensitive to chemotherapy (especially a subset of oligodendrogliomas), while others respond well to radiation therapy.

In choosing a strategy for treating primary brain tumors, both highly malignant and less so, it is of immeasurable benefit to work with a savvy neuro-oncology team. At the Evanston Hospital, I was fortunate to have nationally recognized neuro-oncologists at my side. Most patients with brain tumors were presented at a weekly neuro-oncology conference, where the treatment strategy was discussed. If a biopsy had already been done, the discussion would revolve around whether to proceed with radiation therapy or chemotherapy and in what order if both treatments were indicated. If surgical removal was the consensus, the surgeons would elaborate on the surgical strategy. Such a team approach makes it easier to convey convincingly the recommendation as to the treatment strategy and the prognosis to the patient and family.

The case of a thirty-two-year-old mother of three children with a right frontal-lobe grade II to III oligodendroglioma that presented with seizures exemplifies the benefit of a team effort. The unprecedented large size of the tumor had caused the brain to shift to such a degree that any other choice but a tumor removal would have been extremely dangerous. Proceeding first with a biopsy in order to find out the exact nature of the tumor would have caused just enough additional swelling for the brain functions to decompensate with unfortunate neurologic consequences. Even if a biopsy had succeeded, the radiation and chemotherapies would have been contraindicated due to their tendency to initially cause more swelling and to have delayed effectiveness. At operation, the tumor was removed along with a significant segment of the frontal lobe in the hope of leaving as few of the tumor cells behind as possible, meandering in the process around the anterior cerebral artery and its branches so as to keep them out of harm's way and prevent a stroke. The patient did beautifully and woke up in the recovery room with no focal deficits. The histological and molecular biology examination of the tumor specimen revealed a malignant oligodendroglioma of the variety that is sensitive to chemotherapy. Therefore, under the considered care of the neuro-oncology team, the patient underwent first chemotherapy and subsequently radiation therapy. She was still alive twelve years after surgery, well beyond the average survival of three and a half to four years for patients who are not sensitive to chemotherapy.

PILOCYTIC ASTROCYTOMA

There is a particular subset of primary brain tumors, known as pilocytic astrocytomas that are rather benign and, contingent on their location, amenable to surgical cure. Unfortunately, they can also arise in areas where a surgical removal is not possible (as in the region of the optic nerves and optic nerve crossing, the chiasm) or areas associated with a high potential for complications (as in the hypothalamus or the brain stem).

Early in my professional life, I was asked to see M, an eight-year-old girl who was brought to the emergency department after suffering a grand mal seizure. The grand mal seizure was preceded by two weeks of intermittent focal seizures during which the patient exhibited involuntary forceful turning of her eyes, head, and neck toward the left side. The history of focal seizures preceding a grand mal seizure was consistent with the diagnosis of a brain tumor, at least until proven otherwise. The pattern of the focal seizures suggested that the suspected brain tumor was in the right side of her brain. M, a freckled, soft-spoken girl whose reddish hair was plaited into two pigtails above her ears, was awake and frightened. Her distraught parents stood by her bedside. After a brief introduction and a few soothing words, I proceeded to examine her. Even though M moved all four limbs, the neurological examination showed that she had a mild weakness in her left arm and leg, as they tended to drift down rather promptly with gravity after I asked her to keep them stretched out. The examination also revealed a decreased ability to recognize objects, such as a key, when I placed them in her left hand—a symptom usually referred to as a loss of stereognosis. She also had a dense loss of peripheral vision in her left visual field. The latter two findings suggested that the location of the pathology was probably more toward the posterior segments of the right cerebral hemisphere. M was seen before the availability of the CT scan and long before the MRI era. The only noninvasive imaging study available was a radionuclide scan. This scan showed a dark blotch approximately two inches in diameter, consistent with a tumor, in the right parietal area of the head. After a night in the intensive care unit to stabilize her, M also underwent a cerebral angiogram, which confirmed the presence of a tumor in the parietal area, partially imbedded in the right lateral ventricle. Clearly, M was in trouble, and I had to break the bad news to her distraught parents.

In spite of my choosing the most solicitous words, the parents were understandably devastated. I laced my message with words of encouragement. "The good news is that M's tumor is positioned so that we can operate with a minimal danger of causing loss of speech or memory," I said. "Besides, there is a chance that it may not be malignant." It also did not help when the treating pediatrician began to question the diagnosis and my recommendation to proceed with surgery. After consulting a neurosurgeon on staff at the Children's Memorial Hospital in Chicago, the parents ultimately decided to have the surgery performed by me.

We chose to approach the tumor through the parietal lobe, considering this was the shortest route to the tumor and in view of the already-present parietal lobe symptoms of the losses of the position and localization senses in her left hand. After incising the attenuated cortex in the depth of the groove separating the two adjacent parietal lobe hillocks for a distance of about a centimeter and a half and traversing the underlying white matter, we encountered the tumor at a depth of an inch. The striking difference in appearance between the stark white matter of the brain and the greenish, reddish surface of the tumor made it easy to identify the tumor margins. The size of the tumor and its proximity deep in the brain to the lateral ventricle, which is rich in blood vessels, precluded removing the tumor in one piece, as any attempt to do so could have easily resulted in a hemorrhage. Therefore, we resorted to the well-proven strategy of first reducing the size of the tumor by removing the interior of the tumor before venturing around it. This proved easier than expected, as the tumor core was soft, partially cystic, and relatively void of blood vessels. With the tumor reduced in size, we proceeded to separate the tumor surface from the surrounding brain. The operating microscope is a valuable tool to that end, as it helps identify the undulating interface between the tumor and the brain's white matter. The interface between the tumor and the white matter is not necessarily spherical but instead contains numerous crevasses where the tumor is insinuated deeper into the white matter, requiring intermittently going back into the tumor interior to reduce further the tumor size. Keeping the separated interface between the tumor surface and the white matter open with moist cotton pads, we gradually surrounded the tumor from all sides, which gave us the opportunity to detach it from its root in the depth of the brain. At this point, we had to decide how to detach the tumor from its somewhat-indistinct root. Leaving some of the root behind would risk leaving tumor cells with the potential for a recurrence. On the other hand, removing the root completely together with a segment of the ventricular wall could cause complications, such as a hemorrhage or brain fluid leakage due to a possible failure of the surgically created window in the ventricular wall to heal. Considering M's age and the histological examination of a sample of the tumor removed at the beginning of the operation, which was consistent with pilocytic astrocytoma, we chose the latter strategy as being more promising for a cure. Fortunately, both complications could be avoided. M did rather well after surgery, with only a partial residual defect persisting in her left peripheral visual field. Over the years, M had numerous follow-up imaging studies, including MRIs, without evidence of a recurrence. I chose to describe M's case as a reminder that not all primary brain tumors are incurable and that all patients deserve a chance.

THE STORY OF PITUITARY TUMORS

Triggered by the fellowship in Montreal, I also developed a career-long interest in the surgical treatment of pituitary gland tumors. The pituitary gland is a kidney-bean-sized structure situated in a bony cup known as the sella, in the middle of the skull base, about four inches behind the root of the nose. The pituitary gland is often referred to as the master gland since it regulates the function of other endocrine glands, including the thyroid, adrenal glands, ovaries, and testicles. The pituitary gland also regulates the thirst mechanism, human growth, and a number of other metabolic processes. It does so by producing a variety of hormones that are secreted directly into the bloodstream. The function of the pituitary gland itself is in turn regulated by the brain via a tiny connecting channel known as the pituitary stalk, which transmits hormonal messages from the brain to the pituitary.

As their name implies, pituitary tumors originate from the cell population of the pituitary gland. These are benign, runaway growths of pituitary cell lines that initially form small nodules usually referred to as microadenomas. Some of the nodules enlarge, forming macroadenomas, which can become rather sprawling. If the tumor consists of cells that produce a specific hormone, the bloodstream will be flooded with an excess of that hormone, causing untoward symptoms and signs, usually referred to as a hypersecreting syndrome or disease. Among the hypersecreting syndromes are hyperprolactinemia, acromegaly, and Cushing's disease.

Hyperprolactinemia is the consequence of a hypersecretion of the hormone prolactin, which regulates milk secretion from breasts. Besides symptoms such as headaches and malaise, hyperprolactinemia results in inappropriate milk secretion, loss of menstrual cycle, and infertility in women and a loss of libido in men. The treatment can be medical, with drugs that suppress prolactin secretion, or surgical, designed to remove the tumor. The operation is more successful when the pituitary tumor is of the micro variety.

Acromegaly is caused when the pituitary tumor produces excess amounts of the growth hormone. Acromegaly shortens life because it promotes conditions such as hypertension, cardiac disease, and diabetes. If acromegaly occurs in an adolescent, the patient will also experience excessive growth, usually referred to as gigantism. When acromegaly develops in an adult patient, it causes enlargement and coarsening of facial features, hands, and feet; arthritic changes in joints; carpal tunnel syndrome; an increased tendency toward profuse sweating; and other symptoms, as well as peripheral neuropathies. While there are medications that lessen the symptoms of acromegaly, the preferred treatment is to remove the growth-hormone-secreting tumor. A successful removal of a growth-hormone-producing tumor results in an almost immediate decrease in soft tissue swellings (such as of the tongue, lips, hands, and feet), although it might take several years for a reductive remodeling of the enlarged skeleton to take place.

Cushing's disease is caused by a pituitary tumor that produces excess amounts of a hormone known by the acronym ACTH, which in turn stimulates the adrenal gland to produce increased amounts of cortisone. If left untreated, Cushing's disease is lethal, as it also causes hypertension, cardiac disease, and diabetes. In addition, Cushing's disease manifests with symptoms such as severe malaise; redistribution of fat tissue to the trunk and face (often referred to as the "moon face" and "buffalo hump"), leaving the extremities thin and weakened; weakening bones and spontaneous fractures; excessive facial hair growth; and a tendency toward easy bruising. The treatment is largely surgical, with the goal of removing the hypersecreting pituitary tumor in its entirety while preserving the remainder of the normally functioning gland. As in prolactin-secreting and growth-hormone-secreting tumors, the chances for a surgical cure are much better when the pituitary tumor is of a micro variety. When successful, the operation results not only in a normalization of ACTH and cortisone secretion but also in a conspicuous reversal of symptoms. The improvement, in terms of both appearance and the patient's well-being, can be especially demonstrative. The thrill experienced by the neurosurgeon at having conquered this dreadful disease pales in comparison to the unbridled joy felt by the patient who was given his or her life back.

The majority of pituitary tumors, though, are hormonally silent, meaning they are usually detected at a later stage in their development, when they present either with symptoms of pituitary gland malfunction, such as extreme fatigue, or with symptoms caused by their sheer size. Most commonly, a large pituitary tumor will exert pressure on the crossing of the optic nerves, known as the chiasm, which lies directly above the pituitary gland, causing initially a loss of peripheral vision; if left untreated, it can lead to blindness. The vision loss usually starts inconspicuously and progresses insidiously, although it can occur rapidly, in conjunction with severe headaches, secondary to a spontaneous hemorrhage into the tumor.

The surgical indications and the preoperative workup require collaboration between endocrinologists, ophthalmologists, neuroradiologists, and neurosurgeons. More recently, since the introduction of endoscopic techniques, endoscopy-trained otolaryngologists have been added to the team as well. Transnasal pituitary surgery is based on the notion that the surgical approach to pituitary tumors through the nasal passages is less invasive and safer than opening the skull via a craniotomy. The main reason for this is the precarious intricacy of the anatomy surrounding the sella and a pituitary tumor. The sella lies underneath the crossing of the optic nerves. Guarding the sella on either side like stout serpents are the carotid arteries, the main lifelines to the brain. Just above the sella and chiasm, the carotid arteries branch into ever-smaller caliber arteries that supply oxygen and nutrients to the vital centers in the brain. Behind the sella is the brain stem. Sprouting from the brain stem, cranial nerves meander around the carotid arteries like tiny twigs on either side of the sella, en route to the eye sockets, where they innervate muscles that move the eyeballs. It is clear, therefore, that approaching a pituitary tumor from above, via a craniotomy, requires navigating around precious anatomic structures that if injured could result in disastrous complications, including death, a major stroke, blindness, or double vision.

The only aspect of a pituitary tumor that can be accessed freely and safely is therefore at the bottom of the tumor, through the sella floor, which is usually expanded and thinned by the tumor. Surgeons recognized this anatomic detail at the beginning of the twentieth century. They proposed approaching pituitary tumors from below, through the nasal passages and the centrally placed sphenoid sinus cavity, a procedure that is today commonly called the transsphenoidal operation. Alas, the procedure was short lived, as it fell into disrepute because of complications caused by working in a narrow, deep, and dark surgical corridor at the end of which the tumor could barely be seen with one eye, negating the benefit and comfort of binocular vision. It was not until the introduction of the operating microscope in the early 1960s by Dr. Jules Hardy in Montreal that the transsphenoidal approach once again replaced the craniotomy procedure, this time for good. The reason for such a shift in the operative paradigm was that in addition to the brilliant illumination and magnification, the operating microscope made it possible to view the operative field in a binocular, three-dimensional fashion. This technical innovation made the transnasal approach eminently safer and more effective. More recently, endoscopic techniques have begun to replace the microscope during transsphenoidal operations. In contrast to the microscope, with its preset distance between the objective lens and the operative field, the endoscope lens can be introduced into the operative field at different distances, allowing for variable magnification and a 360-degree panoramic view, albeit in two dimensions only.

Having personally performed close to two thousand transsphenoidal operations using the operating microscope, I gradually streamlined the execution of this procedure. Nevertheless, as with other neurosurgical procedures, the transsphenoidal operation should never be taken lightly, as in each case, there is just enough variation in normal anatomy and in tumor geography to require utmost attention to detail. A meta-analysis of the world literature in 1997 revealed that the frequency of complications from transsphenoidal surgery was with statistical significance directly related to the neurosurgeons' experience: the greater the neurosurgeons' experience, the lesser the probability of a complication. This also holds true relative to the fundamental goals of the operation: endocrine cure in microadenomas (metaphorically, the operation amounts to removing a pea from inside a kidney bean without damaging the bean) and a complete or (if this proves impossible) at least meaningful removal of a large tumor, with relief of pressure against the optic nerves and chiasm. It has always been thrilling to witness a rapid visual recovery reported by the patient, oftentimes the morning after a successfully performed surgery. Yet the elated feeling in the wake of successful operations can be tempered and muted by the failure to accomplish the stated goals and by complications in some patients. The sinking feeling of finding out that the vision has deteriorated after surgery is devastating and unforgettable. Most of the time, visual deterioration was the consequence of inadequate tumor removal, with the remaining tumor tissue swelling up due to surgical manipulations or due to a hemorrhage occurring immediately after the completion of the operation.

Every pituitary neurosurgeon dreads injuring the carotid

arteries that surround the tumor on both sides. Working under a high-power microscopic magnification, I was patiently trying to peel off a growth-hormone-secreting microadenoma from the thin membrane separating the tumor from the right carotid artery, when a sudden, torrential hemorrhage instantly flooded the operative field and beyond. The heart-stopping terror I felt is difficult to put into words, yet I realized that panic would get us nowhere and that my staying calm and thinking clearly were this woman's only hope. My only option was to apply pressure over the point of bleeding by applying layers of moist cotton pads one on top of the other until the sheer weight of the cotton compressed the carotid artery sufficiently to stop the bleeding. While still anesthetized, the patient was taken to the radiology suite where an angiogram confirmed the location of the injury. The carotid artery was occluded with a tiny balloon introduced into the artery with a system of catheters threaded through the circulation from an entry point in the groin. Fortunately, the patient did not suffer a stroke, as the left carotid artery took over supplying the right side of the brain through a system of arterial channels connecting the right and left carotid circulations. The vivid memory of this operation will never fade and will forever leave me with a shivering feeling of utter misery.

BIRCH STREET

After a decade of living on Spruce Street, our family moved to a larger home on the southeast corner of Sunset and Birch Streets, also in Winnetka. Why the move? The reason was in part that Anne wanted our children to attend New Trier East High School, which is nationally recognized for its scholastic achievements. In addition, the development of Skokie Playfields across the street from the Spruce Street home brought along a disturbingly raised noise level from the nightly baseball games and increased traffic on Hibbard Road. Even though the house on Birch Street was one of the oldest in Winnetka, it needed relatively little remodeling, some of which was done by Anne and the girls. From the elevated stoop at the middle of a finely graveled semicircular driveway, one entered a foyer with high ceilings, from which a winding staircase led to the five upstairs bedrooms. From the foyer, double French doors opened straight into a spacious library, in which our family spent most of its leisure time. To the left of the foyer was the dining room, partially paneled in dark wood, and to the right, one entered through an incongruously small arcade into a splendid living room with a large bay window. On the south side of the living room was a summer porch, which we removed and replaced with an elevated patio secluded from the street by ancient oak trees but widely open to the beautifully landscaped yard dominated by the immaculate greenness of the lawn. The beauty of the yard could also be appreciated when viewed through two large floor-to-ceiling French doors along the east wall of the living room. The rooms were exquisitely suited for Anne's collection of Persian carpets and her graceful French antique furniture, including a baby grand piano dating to the classical period of the early 1800s. Overall, the house exuded an air of understated elegance and was suited for entertaining. Over the years, Anne and I established many new friendships that transcended professional acquaintanceships and courtesies. Since these reminiscences are not intended to be a mirror of Anne's and my social life, I ask our closest friends and my numerous colleagues, locally and nationwide, to whom I owe an immense debt of gratitude for their friendship and support, for forgiveness for not singling them out individually. These were also trying years for Anne and me, as we had our share of health issues, including that we are both cancer survivors.

My practice grew in part due to its word-of-mouth reputation, especially since I was treating a number of physicians on the staff and their families, and in part due to a vibrant peer referral base in the domain of pituitary, brain, and skull-base tumor surgery. I also continued to be engaged academically and advanced to the rank of a full professor in the department of neurosurgery at the Northwestern University Feinberg School of Medicine. For what it is worth, I attribute my clinical and academic success in large measure to keeping abreast of the cutting-edge developments in the areas of my professional focus and continuing personal research and innovations that I presented at national meetings and through publications. All along, I shared my enthusiasm for building on the old and learning the new with my residents. I consider having mentored some one hundred future neurosurgeons as one of the greatest privileges of my professional life. My mentees responded in kind when Northwestern University's department of neurosurgery presented me with a lifetime achievement award upon my retirement and established the Ivan S. Ciric Excellence in Teaching Award. In time, I became a member of a number of professional societies, which included the benefit of traveling with Anne, occasionally with the family in tow, to conferences in the United States and abroad.

Upon the passing of my senior associate, Joe Tarkington, in 1988, I assumed the leadership mantle of the division of neurosurgery at Evanston Hospital. In doing so, I also became the holder of the Arlene and Marshall Bennett and Joseph Tarkington Chair of Neurosurgery, which was originally endowed by a grateful patient of Joe's, Mr. Marshall Bennett, who in time became a trusted friend. During my tenure as the division chief, I was surrounded by a highly respected team of neurosurgeons whose expertise, professionalism, and highest ethical standards were acclaimed by our peers nationwide. Ted Eller, an outstanding general and vascular neurosurgeon known for his utmost wisdom and carefulness (who received his stripes via Harvard, Northwestern, and the Mayo Clinic), joined the practice in the late 1970s. Ted is a gentleman with strong convictions who is, however, also inclined toward self-effacing, diplomatic solutions of contentious issues. It is not surprising, therefore, that he was chosen as my successor when I stepped down from leading the division of neurosurgery in 2001. Jeff Cozzens, who trained at Northwestern, joined our practice in the early 1980s. Jeff is a resolute and explicitly communicative person prone to openly revealing his opinions. Jeff is a master surgeon who never shirks from accepting challenging neuro-surgical problems and finding solutions for many. Jeff's initial interest was in pediatric neurosurgery. However, in time and probably because of the institutional tradition of being the re-ferral center for brain tumors, Jeff's focus gradually shifted in that direction. Jeff was also instrumental, along with Ted, in de-veloping the neurosurgical arm of our movement disorder pro-gram. As a champion of those on the lower rungs of health-care delivery and as an enthusiastic teacher, Jeff was adored by the staff and held in the highest esteem by our nurses and residents. Sami Rosenblatt joined our staff in the early 1990s. Already as a resident, Sami showed clinical and academic interest in skull-base surgery and in pituitary surgery in particular, echoing my own professional interests. This forged a close bond between mentor and mentee. Sami's gentlemanly and overall elegant Old World demeanor and his personal history contributed to the cementing of our bond. I was fortunate to have been able to convince Sami, a splendid surgeon, to join our staff upon com-pletion of his fellowship in skull-base surgery at a renowned Cincinnati neurosurgical center. With Sami at my side and with the help of Dr. Jin Chen Zhao, director of our skull-base laboratory, I began the most academically productive period of my professional life. The latest addition to our team was Dean Karahalios, who came to us via the coveted residency program in Phoenix. There he had ample opportunity to acquire superb training in spinal surgery, which became the centerpiece of his professional life. Dean is a quick-thinking, determined, and discerning individual who is well spoken and brimming with soundly conceived leadership ideas of his own.

For a while, we were a group of busy neurosurgeons in private practice, as were most of the physicians and surgeons on the Evanston Hospital staff. In 1991, Evanston Hospital, which in the meantime had reorganized into a multi-institutional entity under the umbrella of Evanston Northwestern Healthcare, began to recruit a team of surgeons and physicians in a contractual relationship modeled after the majority of university hospitals at that time. In this relationship, a percentage of physicians' income is deferred to the institution, primarily but not exclusively in support of academic activities. In return, the institution provides logistical support to the physicians. I readily embraced the new practice paradigm. While we did lose the freedom of being in private practice, to choose our office venue and staff, to negotiate our own contracts with health-care insurers, and the like, the benefits of being part of a successful, growing enterprise outweighed the downsides.

The increasing demands of my professional life had a somewhat-infelicitous effect on my family life, as I became an absentee father of sorts, spending less time with my children. I admit that my parenting was less than desirable, especially when voicing inconsistent opinions on a variety of issues, such as teenage behavior, fiscal conservatism, and social progressiveness. I like to think that these and similar ambiguities in paternal message might have actually helped our discerning children to meet life's challenges squarely and successfully. More likely, though, Anne's involvement in our children's daily lives and education contributed to their weathering the usual trials of teenage years. After graduating from colleges, our children went on to pursue successful careers in journalism, business, and medicine. The joy Anne and I find today being around our children and their families is the best part of our lives, and it certainly trumps all the true and imagined difficulties in their upbringing.

My mother passed away in 1991 at the age of ninety-one. This happened on the eve of the 1990s' Yugoslav wars. My mother's funeral was attended by a multitude of Karlovci residents, who came to pay their last respects to the person on whose shoulders they'd found comfort and encouragement. The funeral was a solemn occasion. In the cathedral, the mass was officiated by the Karlovci bishop and a retinue of priests attired in their dark purple funeral regalia. After the mass, the clergy and the villagers followed the casket, which was placed on a cart pulled by six friends of the family in a cortege up the hill to the family's burial plot. I will never forget the otherworldly moment of entombment with the bishop and clergy chanting the last prayers as the late-autumn sun was slowly setting behind the surrounding hills, painting crimson the scattered clouds and casting long shadows over the serene scene. After my mother's death, my younger sister, Kitty, remained the guardian of the family traditions.

Back in Belgrade, there was a palpable nationalistic fervor sparked by the national-socialist government in the wake of the beginning of Yugoslavia's demise. It took nine long years of suffering and lost lives before a popular uprising led to Milosevic's overthrow in October of 2000. For Americans of Serbian ancestry the 1990s were a difficult time of coming to grips with reality, when our adoptive country unleashed air strikes over our homeland and our people. This was especially true for those of us who grew up believing that Yugoslavia was a successful union created in the wake of the Great War by the signatories of the Treaty of Versailles. In fact, President Wilson was instrumental to that end, as he convinced other victorious leaders, notably Vittorio Orlando of Italy and Georges Clemenceau of France, both of whom initially opposed formation of a potentially influential state on the Balkan Peninsula, to sign on to the creation of Yugoslavia.

IVAN CIRIC, MD

THE CUTTING EDGE OF SKULL-BASE SURGERY

It has been my impression that casual observers of neurosurgery often assume that neurosurgeons thrive in performing exceptionally rare and challenging operations. Perhaps that is so, but my own experience tells me otherwise. To my thinking, in some ways, neurosurgeons are similar to performance artists, such as musicians or actors. To be sure, both prefer to excel in performing difficult tasks to perfection, something that is rarely accomplished the first time around and usually requires many hours of practice and repeated performances. Only then can they claim virtuosity. My advice to young neurosurgeons over the years, therefore, has been not to perform an occasional, once-in-a-lifetime, uniquely difficult surgery just for the sake of meeting the challenge at best or as a concession to the all-too-pervasive surgeon's ego at worst. I suppose they might be justified in tackling such a challenge if they have specialized training under credible mentorship and are willing to devote the necessary long hours to accomplish the task, preferably in the programmatic setting of a surgical team. Drawing on my own experience as a resident that practicing surgical skills and replicating novel techniques in a laboratory setting facilitates acquisition of surgical expertise in the operating room, I established a microsurgical laboratory at the Evanston Hospital, with six operating microscopes equipped with video capabilities. In this effort, I was fortunate to have the invaluable help of Dr. Jin Chen Zhao, a skilled neuro-otologist. The laboratory was modeled after similar teaching facilities in centers such as Zurich, Switzerland, and Cincinnati, Ohio. Over the years, generations of neurosurgery residents and other surgical specialties were thus able to hone their microsurgical skills, including performing a series of microvascular exercises using the operating microscope and micro techniques. One of the exercises involved reconnecting divided carotid arteries one millimeter in diameter in anesthetized rats by circumferentially placing six sutures that were nearly invisible to the naked eye but gloriously magnified under the microscope without compromising the circulation through the tiny vessels.

As an extension of my interest in microsurgery of pituitary tumors, I also became intrigued early on in my career by the emerging field of skull-base surgery for other tumors arising along the skull base. During my residency, many of these tumors were off-limits to neurosurgeons, for they were not reachable using the techniques available at that time. Before I continue, it would seem appropriate to revisit the concept of the skull base and to explain the challenge posed by skull-base tumors. I shall start by paraphrasing Dr. Bucy, who used the metaphor of a closed box. Just as a closed box has a lid, sides, and a base, a skull consists of a vault, sides, and a base. Similarly, just as a box can be lined on the inside with felt or some other material, the skull is wallpapered on the inside by a grayish and tough membrane, the previously mentioned dura, which approximates all the niches and crevasses in the skull. Inside, filling the skull box to the brim (especially in younger individuals), is the most precious jewel of them all: the human brain, with its appendages and numerous blood vessels. A translucent sac known as the arachnoid membrane surrounds the brain, its appendages, and the blood vessels. Inside the arachnoid sac, the brain fluid circulates through the brain cavities and around the brain surface. The dura and the arachnoid are cumulatively also known as the meninges. While the base of a box is ordinarily flat, the skull base is a three-tiered bony plate that slopes from the front to the back of the skull. The deepest part of the skull base, also known as the posterior fossa, is, as its name implies, in the back of the skull. The skull base has several openings within it, the largest one being in the center of the posterior fossa, where the skull docks with the spine. Skull-base tumors are mostly benign growths whose histological examination shows a quiescent cell population that resembles the tissue of their origin, with only a few cells undergoing replication. They can be tucked deeply under the brain in a tight space. Considering that the brain fills the skull with little room to spare, it is easy to understand that such growths can exert serious pressure against brain structures in the immediate vicinity of the tumor, such as the cranial nerves and the brain stem. More ominously, skull-base tumors can block brain fluid from flowing through its natural paths within the brain chambers. Such scenarios can lead to disabling symptoms or prove lethal if left untreated.

This short primer on the skull base and skull-base tumors makes it easier to understand that an operation for removal of a large and unwieldy skull-base tumor can be a daunting task that is fraught with difficulties and potentially associated with life-altering complications. Compared to pituitary tumors, exposure and removal of other skull-base tumors, such as craniopharyngiomas, meningiomas, and vestibular schwannomas (to mention the three most common tumor types occurring along the skull base), requires an even greater degree of neurosurgical sophistication and specialized training. One of the fundamentals Dr. Bucy taught his residents was that forcefully elevating, or retracting, the brain in order to reach for a tumor is prohibited, lest a substantial injury occur to the underlying brain tissue. Therefore, instead of undue brain retraction, neurosurgeons have designed a series of ingenious techniques during which parts of the skull base are removed, which brings the surgeon closer to the tumor and hopefully creates just enough room to proceed with the microsurgical tumor removal without the need to forcefully elevate the brain. This is easier said than done, in view of the numerous neural and vascular structures that are either contained within the skull base or passing through it, including the life-sustaining carotid arteries and the all-important cranial nerves, which have to be kept out of harm's way.

In order to shorten the learning curve, neurosurgery residents were instructed in our laboratory in the microsurgical operative approaches to the skull base on cadaver heads commercially available for research and education. I also took every opportunity to rehearse in the laboratory especially intricate operative approaches prior to the actual surgery. Still, as much as the simulation in the laboratory is a desirable experience conducive to mastering the skull-base anatomy, honing microsurgical skills, and acquiring the technical fundamentals of skull-base approaches, it is not sufficient to declare expertise in this highly challenging field of neurosurgery. Expertise is earned in the operating room by performing a given procedure many times over. It takes time, dedication, perseverance, a team approach, and, above all, salutary operative outcomes to build a reputable skull-base surgery practice. In time, our laboratory became a learning center for skull-base approaches for younger neurosurgeons, as Dr. Zhao organized courses during which the participants were instructed in a whole spectrum of microsurgical approaches to the skull base under the guidance of a nationally recognized expert invited as a guest faculty. The mutually converging aspirations by the team members contributed to the success of the endeavor.

Besides the removal of parts of the skull base, there are additional methods that facilitate the approach to a skull-base tumor. These include elevation of the patient's head in relationship to the heart, administration of diuretic agents, decreasing the blood CO_2 content by increasing the depth and rate of respirations, and releasing the cerebrospinal fluid from its pockets around the brain, known as the cisterns, all of which can result in a temporary reduction in brain volume. This allows the brain to recede spontaneously away from the skull base, further opening the corridor to the tumor.

Once a skull-base tumor is reached, its removal is accomplished in accordance with the same principles as described previously. These include a reduction in tumor size before it is removed, and the use of the operating microscope. Decrease in tumor size allows the neurosurgeon to visualize and thus safeguard the neural and vascular structures that are hidden behind the tumor. It is only when the neurosurgeon has these structures in full view that a skull-base tumor can be separated from them safely along an appropriate plane. Under the best of circumstances, in the hands of an experienced skull-base surgeon who is familiar with the complexity of navigating the treacherous terrain of the skull base and supported by a quality team, a complete and safe removal of a skull-base tumor is the goal of the operation. Since a complete removal is not always possible, a portion of the tumor might have to be left behind. Consequently, in such cases, a close follow-up with repeat MRI imaging is necessary in order to detect any evidence of a recurrent growth.

THE CHALLENGE OF CRANIOPHARYNGIOMAS

Considering my interest in the surgery of pituitary tumors, I was also referred patients with craniopharyngiomas, noncancerous but oftentimes unforgiving tumors that arise in the general area of the pituitary gland. They affect primarily children but without sparing adults. In my practice, I have treated adult craniopharyngioma patients only.

The development of craniopharyngiomas is an interesting embryological story that I shall attempt to explain with a few simple words. In the human embryo, the developing brain and the early oral cavity are next to each other. At one point in the gestation, the roof of the oral cavity bubbles up toward the primitive brain to form a pouch, known as the Rathke's pouch. The stem of the pouch eventually closes off, creating thereby a sealed-off Rathke's cyst. The cyst, in turn, gradually evolves into the pituitary gland. In most individuals, the stem of the pouch vanishes toward the end of gestation. In a few persons, however, the cell line of the stem, which is similar to that of the oral cavity, becomes active and begins to multiply. Unlike in the oral cavity, where the dying cells are freely shed, the dying cells in the activated stem have no such avenue for shedding and begin to accumulate as debris, eventually resulting in a growth in the immediate vicinity of the pituitary gland. Since craniopharyngiomas are frequently attached to the base of the brain in the area of the hypothalamus and the pituitary stalk, a complete removal might not be possible, leaving the doors open for the possibility of a recurrence. A close postoperative surveillance with repeat MRI examinations is therefore mandatory. Recently, some neurosurgeons have been advocating focused high-energy-beam radiation therapy at the first sign of a recurrence in adult patients.

I cherished the opportunity to operate on patients with this tricky tumor, most of the time via a craniotomy and occasionally, when so reachable, using the transnasal approach. For a while, I was intrigued by the fact that when operating on these tumors using the transnasal approach, I had a higher incidence of postoperative brain-fluid leaks dripping from the nose compared to the low incidence of this serious complication in patients with pituitary tumors. The answer to that riddle, as to many others, came one day while I was jogging after work. I suppose endorphins help the thought processes besides making one feel well. The answer lay in the distinctly different relationship of pituitary tumors and of craniopharyngiomas to the arachnoid sac, which contains the cerebrospinal fluid. Pituitary tumors are positioned outside the arachnoid membrane, while craniopharyngiomas can have a variable relationship, with many being at least partially inside the arachnoid sac, because of which their removal opens the floodgate for brain fluid to escape. Armed with this knowledge, we were able to improve the operative outcomes in our patients with craniopharyngiomas.

The case of P, a twenty-four-year-old medical student, exemplifies the challenges neurosurgeons face when operating on craniopharyngiomas. The patient became aware of some visual difficulties for the first time about a year prior to my seeing him. For example, he had to sit in the front of the class room in order to be able to see what was written on the blackboard. One day he simply could not decipher the writing on the blackboard, even though he was sitting just in front of it. He was referred to an ophthalmologist, who discovered a severe loss of vision in both eyes, worse in the right eye. He was perilously close to being legally blind. The examination of the visual fields showed a pronounced reduction with only a narrow field of vision persisting. The perceptive ophthalmologist recognized that these findings were likely secondary to a tumor interfering with the optic nerves and the optic nerve crossing (chiasm). He recommended that an urgent MRI of the brain be obtained with special attention to the skull base in the area of the optic nerves. The MRI showed an approximately inch-and-a-half tumor positioned immediately above the sella and the pituitary gland, occupying the space along the skull base usually reserved for the optic nerve crossing. A careful review of the MRI suggested that the optic nerves were severely elevated and stretched by the tumor. The MRI also showed that the tumor had distorted the base of the brain in the region of the previously described third ventricle. In metaphor, one could describe the relationship of the tumor to the brain as that of a plum stuck in the base of a ball of dough. Moreover, the carotid arteries, including one of their main branches (known by the acronym ACA), coursed on the sides and in front of the tumor. Behind the tumor loomed another important artery, known as the basilar artery. Sprouting from these major vessels was a leash of tiny arterial branches that surrounded the tumor circumferentially on their way to nourish the base of the brain. An injury to these so-called per-forating arteries could have disastrous neurologic consequences or be lethal. The MRI appearance of the tumor itself suggested that it contained pockets of fluid interspersed between areas of solid tumor tissue, consistent with a craniopharyngioma.

I was asked to see the patient in an urgent consultation. P was a tall, serious young man who was prematurely balding for his age. He was pale and appeared tired, lacking energy. Obviously, his greatest concern was whether he would become blind. I reassured him that by removing the pressure against his optic nerves, there was a good chance we could save the existing degree of vision, and based on prior experience, the operation might actually lead to a visual recovery. At the same time, I had to tell him in the gentlest way of the possibility that the opera-tion and the sudden release of pressure against the optic nerves could have the opposite effect and that his vision could be worse after surgery. Considering that the patient was a medical stu-dent, I had to adjust my explanations accordingly but also shy away from sounding too technical, especially since his parents had come along for the appointment. I decided that the best way to proceed was to explain the surgical indications, surgical strategy, and possible side effects and complications of surgery in light of the anatomic structures the tumor was surrounded by. We spent more than two hours sitting next to each other, huddling together over a skull and brain model and viewing the magnified images of the MRI. It was my impression that P understood and accepted the seriousness of his situation on an intellectual level, yet on a human level, he was understandably anxious as to his immediate and long-term future.

My surgical strategy was to access the tumor through a

modified skull-base approach whereby we would reach for the tumor from above the right eye socket. This approach requires removal of a portion of the skull base to gain sufficient room underneath the brain for safe surgical manipulations. The alternate path to the tumor would have been to approach the tumor through the transnasal route. Both approaches have advantages and disadvantages. I chose the former strategy since the latter would have been more confining, making it more difficult to remove this large tumor and deal with possible complications.

On the day of surgery, in the preoperative holding area, P was surrounded by his family. He was at peace with the notion of the upcoming surgery as he held my right hand to his heart and looked me straight in the eyes with an encouraging gaze conveying trust and confidence. P's mother interrupted this quiet moment between the surgeon and patient, possibly a future surgeon himself, by exclaiming, "Son, don't hold his hand! I would like to see if his hand shakes." I dutifully extended my right hand, and upon seeing the result, she jokingly declared me as being fit to proceed with surgery. A small infusion of humor is always welcome under such circumstances.

Upon opening the skull and after drilling away part of the skull base, the operating microscope was brought into position for the duration of the operation. The dura was relaxed, under no tension, and we could open it readily and safely. We then proceeded to separate the right frontal and temporal lobes along a natural cleavage plain between the two lobes (known as the Sylvian fissure). This maneuver opened a wide corridor down to the right optic nerve and chiasm. The optic nerve was short and stretched out by the tumor beneath it. The only place we were able to get a glimpse of the brownish-green tumor was along a short, slit-like opening between the optic nerve and the carotid artery, positioned immediately next to the optic nerve. Working patiently under high-power magnification, we also exposed the optic nerve crossing, the left optic nerve, and the area of the brain immediately above the optic nerve crossing, which consists of a thin layer of brain tissue known as the lamina terminalis. In fact, this tissue layer was so thin that we were able to see the greenish hue of the tumor hiding behind it. With the exposure of the operative site completed, we took a few minutes to regroup, discussing our options. Considering that the optic nerves were quite short, there was no room at all between them to try to reach for the tumor. We had the option of drilling away the skull base in front of the optic nerve crossing in order to create the necessary room to reach for the tumor. I decided against that option since the slightest trauma to the optic nerves would have surely led to blindness. Another option was to use the slit-like opening between the right optic nerve and the carotid artery to place a needle into the tumor and aspirate the fluid contained within the tumor cavity. This maneuver would have collapsed the tumor and relieved the pressure against the optic nerves. However, I doubted we would have been able to remove the entire solid part of the tumor and the tumor capsule using this narrow port of entry only, with the overwhelming probability that the tumor would refill with fluid within a matter of weeks, if not days. Finally, there was the option of going through the markedly attenuated lamina terminalis, since the tumor was immediately behind it. Based on our experience with prior similar cases, I reached the decision to combine the latter two options by first aspirating the fluid from the tumor through the above-mentioned slit-like space and then removing the solid part of the tumor through the lamina terminalis. The plan proceeded without a hitch. Immediately upon aspirating about one-third of an ounce of oily fluid, we could see the optic nerves and the chiasm relax so that they were no longer under tension. Opening the lamina terminalis is not a difficult maneuver, although it can be associated with complications, such as an injury to the optic nerve crossing, the hypothalamus, and the surrounding arterial vessels. We managed to avoid these obstacles as we exposed the tumor. After opening the tumor capsule, we were able to remove the yellowish solid part of the tumor, which had the consistency of cottage cheese. With the fluid and the solid component of the tumor removed, the tumor capsule collapsed and began to recede from the optic nerves. As we refocused the microscope on the right optic nerve, we could see that the initially seen slit-like space between the optic nerve and the carotid artery had slightly enlarged as the optic nerve had receded toward the midline once the pressure behind it was relieved.

Removing the tumor capsule not only is the crucial phase of the operation that will define the result in terms of cure versus possibility of recurrence if a part of the capsule is left behind but also is associated with the greatest risks. The reason for this is that a segment of the capsule can be intimately adherent—stuck, in simple terms—to the base of the brain in the region of the hypothalamus, the pituitary stalk, and the arteries coursing nearby. The hypothalamus is a precious territory in the human brain and controls a number of vital functions, such as consciousness; the regulation of sleep, hunger, and thirst; and a host of autonomic functions, from the heart rate to the respiratory cycle. Besides the possibility of imperiled vital signs, including a loss of consciousness, interfering with the hypothalamus and the pituitary stalk can also result in water-wasting syndrome (also known as diabetes insipidus), a serious metabolic consequence that can lead to convulsions. This phase of the operation is also unpredictable because some of the surgical maneuvers are executed inside deep niches and crevasses without direct vision, relying only on the surgeon's tactile sense.

Considering that the tumor capsule could be easily separated from the optic nerves and chiasm as well as from the carotid arteries under direct vision with the microscope, I felt that we should try to peel the capsule off the base of the brain as well. As much as I tried to visualize the interface between the tumor capsule and the base of the brain using the operating microscope, I was unable to do so due to the angle of the visual axis. The endoscope equipment was also not suited for such an endeavor. We did use a small mirror the size of a dime, which we introduced underneath the brain to inspect the relationship of the tumor capsule to the surrounding structures, unfortunately without benefitting from the maneuver, as the mirror fogged up as soon as it came in contact with brain fluid. In short, from this point on, I had to rely on my tactile sense as I began removing the tumor capsule. Any sensation of resistance to peeling the tumor capsule off the base of the brain had to be heeded as a warning sign that the capsule might be attached either to the hypothalamus and the pituitary stalk or to a major vessel. With my respirations shallower and my heartbeat slower for what seemed to be an eternity, I gradually eased the tumor capsule out from underneath the brain. I knew that we had removed the back end of the tumor capsule when the pituitary stalk came into view, coursing through the empty space once occupied by the tumor.

For a while, I just sat there quietly on my stool, taking deep breaths and thanking Providence for this young man's life. We were not finished yet, for there was still the business of closing the craniotomy wound, with all of its pitfalls that can create havoc in the immediate postoperative period. Some surgeons leave the operating room at this point, delegating the execution of the closure phase of the operation to their residents. Whether out of personal insecurity or because I was reluctant to delegate responsibility in my patients, I remained in the operating room until the skin was closed. My resident and I simply switched chairs, with me assisting in the closure.

P woke up in the recovery room with his vision unchanged, perhaps slightly better, and with no new neurologic deficits. Within a matter of days, his vision began to improve noticeably. A year after surgery, the only residual visual problem was a loss of peripheral vision in the upper outer quadrant of his right visual field. As for any metabolic changes, he did develop temporary diabetes insipidus, which was easily treated by the consulting endocrinologist, who also shored up P's lack of testosterone production. Free of a recurrence of his tumor, my patient finished medical school and embarked on a successful medical career. The privilege of being this young colleague's surgeon has enriched my life.

Unfortunately, operating on craniopharyngiomas can also be associated with poor outcomes. Such was the case with a forty-five-year-old man with a long history of weight gain and the recent onset of headaches, unsteadiness, and progressive memory loss. It was not until the patient was involved in an accident, having fallen asleep at the wheel of his car, that the reason behind his symptoms was discovered. In the emergency room of a local hospital, a CT scan and subsequent MRI showed a large tumor with the imaging characteristics of a craniopharyngioma occupying the significantly enlarged midline brain chamber, the third ventricle. The tumor had also spread into the right lateral ventricle. Both the right and the left lateral ventricles were enlarged because of a partial blockage to the brain fluid circulation. Without going into a debate as to the possible surgical and nonsurgical treatment options and the appropriateness of my surgical strategy, let me just say that I chose to approach and remove this tumor from above, between the two brain hemispheres. I executed the plan to a T, with the caveat that the tumor was intimately attached to the walls and floor of the third ventricle, the hypothalamus, with which it blended imperceptibly and that it had splayed apart and thinned out the main memory circuits. The intimate relationship between the tumor and the hypothalamus made it difficult to find a plane of cleavage between them, and as a result, a complete removal was not possible. Postoperatively, the patient remained unconscious for several weeks. As he finally began to respond, he remained sluggish, drifting into sleep at every opportunity. He had no immediate memory recall—he could not remember having seen his wife five minutes previously—and he lost his thirst mechanism, which was a serious handicap in light of his excessive urination, which left him trending toward crippling dehydration. He also developed a voracious appetite and gained weight rapidly, which made it even more difficult for the nursing and physical therapy staffs to overcome his resistance to being mobilized out of bed and into a chair, let alone to walking.

THE CROSSING

Anne, who grew up surrounded by the hills of the Black Forest, managed to convert me from a beach bum and useless sun worshipper to a devoted hiker and skier. While the kids were still at home, the family would go to Colorado for a week of skiing. We enjoyed the European atmosphere in Vail, the friendliness of Keystone, the chance to rub shoulders with the rich and famous in Telluride, and the Victorian ambience of Aspen. During one of the sojourns at Aspen, a skier ran into Anne (of all places, on the innocent slopes of the Buttermilk). Anne somersaulted down the mountain, losing the skis and landing on her back, fracturing her second lumbar vertebra. Fortunately, the fall did not cause any neurologic injury. Six months in a body brace healed the fracture. This was the end of skiing for Anne but not the end of our love for the Colorado Rockies, in winter or summer. After the children went off to colleges, Anne and I continued spending time enjoying the enchanting winter scenes at Vail. I would sneak in a run or two of skiing, but mostly, we did some serious snowshoeing up the slopes to the summit. After a leisurely breakfast, we would take a shortcut to the slopes (along a street with mansions where dogs are named Caviar and Champagne), where we would get into our snowshoes and head up the Gitalong Trail toward Mid-Vail. Skiers swooshing by would occasionally yell obscenities at us. I responded in kind—but only after they were some ten yards down the slope. After a rest and lunch, it would be off to the summit at 11,800 feet for a cup of hot tea. The view from Eagle's Nest Ridge is incredibly spectacular, with the imposing snowcapped peaks encircling the horizon. Tired and thrilled that we had managed to complete the hike, we would catch the gondola down to Lion's Head. I was in pretty good shape, but snowshoeing trumps all other exercises.

For a number of years, Anne and I went to Vail also in the summer. There was no shortage of hiking trails. On one occasion, we lost our bearings while on poorly marked Upper Piney Trail. Luckily, the setting sun, the emerging moon, and Anne's good sense of orientation bailed us out. On another occasion, we managed to hike up Holy Cross Mountain in the Sawatch Range. The trail, which started at 9,500 feet, appeared bucolic at the beginning, as it wound along meadows and pine forests. Soon, though, we were above the tree line, along craggy and steep switchbacks. Anne, the consummate alpinist, treaded lightly. By the time we reached the summit, I had no energy to muster for the last hundred steps to a hut, anticipating all kinds of cardiac emergencies.

I do not remember what prompted us to change our allegiance from Vail and the Colorado Rockies to Santa Fe and the Pecos wilderness of the Sangre de Cristo Range surrounding it. Anne was always interested in the history of Native American culture and in the stories of dark and iniquitous subjugation of the ancient Native American civilization by the Spanish conquistadores and the messianic and oftentimes-belligerent spread of Christianity. *Willa Cather's Death Comes for the Archbishop*, a beautifully written novel about the life of the first bishop of Santa Fe, Jean Marie Latour, also enthralled both of us. Thus, it was off to Santa Fe.

The first time we went, we flew into Albuquerque and drove to Santa Fe. At the outskirts of the town we were greeted by a short albeit torrential rainstorm that unleashed thunder and lightning, forebodingly illuminating the dark skies. In the wake of the short storm, which also featured hail, there appeared in the clearing skies multiple rainbows of such vivid colors, as we had never seen. After settling in at the Inn of the Anasazi, we explored the city, admiring the adobe-style buildings, beautifully complementing the southwestern landscape. We loved the city, with its culinary delights and cultural diversions, and even more, we loved the surrounding Native American territories. We chose different routes of reaching the city and leaving it, driving through New Mexico's cities and villages—through Taos, Los Alamos, and Gallup and into the neighboring northeast Arizona through the Navajo and Hopi lands. On one occasion, we stayed at Chinle on our way to the moonscape-like Canyon de Chelly, with its barely accessible and abandoned Hopi adobes carved into the vertical cliffs of the canyon.

On this and many subsequent occasions, we went hiking in the mountains surrounding Santa Fe. There are three peaks just outside Santa Fe (Baldy, Lake Peak, and Penitente Peak), all of them around twelve thousand feet. We learned that there is a crossing along a narrow ridge between Lake Peak and Penitente Peak, with precipices on either side of the ridge, making walking along it hazardous for those squeamish of heights and unsure of footing. A colleague of mine who made the crossing did so crawling on his knees. Well, we were not about to be denied such excitement, not to mention the time we would save coming down the other side instead of turning around along the same trail. We were at the summit of Lake Peak, looking at the crossing and pondering our next steps, when a storm came upon us out of the blue sky. We ran toward a shack close by, when lightning struck the ground immediately next to me. It threw me to the ground, and for a moment, I was stunned, dazed. Anne ran toward me to help me up, and I shouted that she should continue toward the shack. The shack was filled with other hikers. It turned out that they were scientists from nearby Los Alamos, and they discussed the physics of lightning in high altitude. We listened to their discourse with interest, but mostly, we were relieved to have escaped from a near disaster. Of course, that crossing would have to wait.

In our second attempt to make the crossing, we changed our strategy. We decided to make the crossing from the Penitente Peak side to Lake Peak. We took off early in the morning on a picture-perfect, calm, cool day in late August. After we meandered through pine forests and crossed several mountain streams, the trail emerged on a large meadow, the Puerto Nambe plain. It was noon by the time we stepped onto the grassy embankment of Puerto Nambe, and the sun was at its zenith. Clearly, hiking up the treeless Baldy, just to our left, was out of the question, so we forged on up the forested trail toward Penitente. It was around three o'clock in the afternoon by the time we reached the slope above the tree line. We reached the summit, admiring the vistas and staying away from the seemingly oblivious mountain sheep grazing around. Alas, we searched for the entrance to the crossing to Lake Peak in vain. We could see Lake Peak just a stone's throw away, but it seemed there was no crossing. Time passed in the futile search until it was getting late. With no other choice, we grudgingly turned around. Night came upon us while we were still on the trail. We had enough water and energy bars in our backpacks but had no gear to fend off the chill of the night. Anne seemed unperturbed. When I inquired as to her nonchalance, she reminded me that this was the night of a full moon. Indeed, the friendly face of the moon appeared soon in the star-studded sky, giving us plenty of light to follow the trail down to our car.

Disappointed but not disillusioned, we drove into town for a consolation steak dinner, of course with a glass of wine for Anne and a martini for me, in one of our favorite eateries, the Palace Restaurant and Saloon, where one mingles with the local ranchers, cowboys, and lovely Santa Fe maidens. Delightful!

THE TRICKY ALLURE OF SKULL-BASE MENINGIOMAS

Meningiomas are among the most common benign intra-cranial tumors. As their name implies, meningiomas arise from the meninges, specifically from small protrusions of the arachnoid membrane that are buried within the dura. While overwhelmingly benign when examined under the pathologist's microscope, skull-base meningiomas can behave aggressively, as they tend to invade the dura and even the skull bone, so a complete removal is at times difficult to accomplish.

My interest in skull-base meningiomas was sparked by a subset of these tumors, known as tuberculum sellae meningiomas, which originate on the skull base immediately in front of the sella and the pituitary gland. They frequently interfere with the optic nerves and optic nerve crossing (chiasm), resulting in visual symptoms similar to those caused by large pituitary tumors. Since I had the reputation of being a pituitary surgeon, patients harboring these tumors were referred to my clinic. In contrast to pituitary tumors, most of the tuberculum sellae meningiomas require a craniotomy, although recently, neurosurgeons have gathered the courage and acquired enough know-how to approach these tumors transnasally as well. While challenging, removal of these tumors is largely associated with excellent results. I enjoyed operating on these tumors and reported my results in the neurosurgical literature. Meningiomas, though, can arise any place along the skull base, where they can encircle structures such as the carotid arteries and their branches, cranial nerves, and the like, making an attempt to remove them completely hazardous.

I will always remember the forty-six-year-old woman who had a history of seizures and whose MRI showed a large meningioma underneath the frontal and temporal lobes of the brain. The deep side of the tumor straddled the right optic nerve and the adjacent carotid artery. While challenging, this tumor was nevertheless eminently accessible through a variant of a skull-base approach known as the pterional approach. After we labored for several hours to decrease the tumor size by coring out its interior, the tumor capsule became less taut, permitting us to separate meticulously the capsule from the frontal and temporal lobes and to free the optic nerve. In my desire to go to the limit, I attempted to peel off the last vestiges of the meningioma in the very depth of the exposure, only to cause a tear in the carotid artery to which the tumor was intimately attached. To witness the fountain of blood gushing from a torn carotid artery is a spine-chilling experience, to say the least. Such a cataclysmic event requires the immediate lifesaving measures of occlusion of the vessel upstream from the tear, followed in short order by either a primary repair of the tear or a bypass operation in which a vascular graft is inserted into the carotid artery that circumvents the tear. These maneuvers have to be executed swiftly under the time constraint of brain tolerance for ischemia. If these measures fail or are deemed unworkable, a mere shutting off of the carotid artery will result in a major stroke unless there are collateral vessels downstream from the tear that bring blood to the deprived side of the brain from the opposite carotid circulation. There was no blame to pass around; there was no exculpatory explanation, such as if I had not used the operating microscope. It was a simple defiance of the old wisdom that judgment is the better part of valor.

As it turned out, the patient did develop a stroke, leaving her with a weakness in her left extremities that improved somewhat with physical therapy but from which she never recovered completely. Considering that the stroke involved the nondominant right side of the brain, the speech centers remained unaffected, giving her the opportunity to rightfully (although not scathingly so) scold me whenever she came for a follow-up visit. Yet this nice woman was also pleased that the follow-up MRI studies remained negative for any residual or recurrent tumor, signifying cure. The alternative strategy in this patient would have been to leave a small residual cuff of meningioma tissue attached to the carotid artery, follow up with repeat MRI studies at regular intervals, and proceed with radiation to the residual tumor using the high-energy focused beam technique at the first sign of a recurrence.

While this insalubrious outcome occurred in a patient with an eminently approachable meningioma because of a desire to achieve a complete removal, there are also skull-base meningiomas that are truly difficult to access, let alone remove. Specifically, a meningioma that arises directly in front of the brain stem, along the portion of the skull base known as the clivus, requires a complex tactical removal of the skull base, including a technique whereby the tumor is reached through the oral cavity. The removal of a meningioma in that location is difficult, because the tumor frequently envelops the main feeding artery to the brain stem, the basilar artery, and its branches, known as the perforators. This makes an attempt to remove such a tumor a nearly impossible task, as even the gentlest manipulation of the severely stretched perforator vessels can cause a brain stem stroke, resulting in a variety of symptoms, such as paralysis, loss of consciousness, and even death. This is precisely what happened to a seventy-two-year-old woman who had progressing symptoms of difficulty with swallowing and unsteadiness. An MRI revealed a large tumor that had the imaging characteristics of a meningioma directly underneath the brain stem. Considering her symptoms, especially the difficulty with swallowing (even of her saliva, which eventually would have led to bouts with pneumonia), we were in a quandary, stuck between a rock and a hard place regarding how to proceed from there. One option was to go for tumor removal, if only partially, to relieve the pressure against the brain stem. On the other hand, we also considered not intervening at all in view of the uncertainty as to the outcome of the operation. After repeated discussions with the patient, husband, and a daughter, the consensus was to proceed with surgery. Without describing the procedure, let me just say that the patient never woke up after surgery and had to be placed on life support, including assisted respirations. Shortly thereafter, the patient developed pneumonia, and her organ systems began to fail. In keeping with the patient's explicit desire not to be kept on life support, the family, the patient's internist, and the consulting neurologist decided to withhold further treatment.

The difference between doable and nondoable and between

cure and death in skull-base meningiomas is at times measured in millimeters. For example, if the afore-described tumor had been off toward one side, displacing sideways rather than elevating the brain stem, not enveloping the basilar artery circumferentially but perhaps only partially, removal of such a meningioma, while still requiring a complex strategy and a team effort, could have been successful. This brings us to the case of N.

N was a lovely lady in her early thirties who was referred to me because of a several-months-long history of progressive unsteadiness, clumsiness in her left arm and hand, and numbness in the right side of her face. Her MRI showed an elongated football-shaped meningioma of approximately two and a half inches in greatest diameter compressing the brain stem from the right side to half of its normal size. Before I proceed with a brief discussion of the operation, I should add another bit of explanatory information regarding the anatomy of the skull base. The posterior fossa, which we have visited previously, is partitioned from the rest of the skull cavity by a tent-shaped sheet of dura known as the tentorium. Resting on the tentorium above is the back end of the brain, the occipital lobe, and below it is the small of the brain, the cerebellum. The tentorium has an approximately one-inch-wide opening to accommodate the brain stem as it passes from the skull compartment above the tentorium into the posterior fossa en route to connect with the spinal cord. This patient's meningioma arose precisely at the right margin of the opening in the tentorium. As it grew, the meningioma had mercilessly compressed the brain stem within the rigid confines of the opening in the tentorium. The surgical strategy chosen by our skull-base team, based on similar successfully operated cases in the past, was to access the tumor using a combined approach from above and behind the right ear. This strategy also required a partial removal of the right inner ear bone, all with the goal of isolating and removing the right side of the tentorium, a tricky maneuver that would open a surgical corridor between the temporal lobe and cerebellum and bring us close to the tumor.

With the craniotomies completed the neuro-otologist entered the operative field and proceeded to perform a partial removal of the inner ear bone, a procedure known as retrolabyrinthine petrosectomy. He carefully navigated his drill through the complex maze of the inner ear bone in order to prevent deafness in the right ear and paralysis of the right side of the face.

The next step was to open the dura above and below the tentorium. This maneuver isolated the lateral margin of the tentorium, which we then divided down to the tumor, taking care to safeguard the fourth cranial nerve that runs along the inner margin of the tentorium. An injury to that nerve would have resulted in permanent double vision. Meanwhile, brain fluid was released from the surrounding cisterns, adding to the brain relaxation. The cumulative effect of these maneuvers was that we were facing the tumor at the bottom of a wide corridor between the temporal lobe and the cerebellum.

I reviewed the operative field under the microscope. Magnified and glistening under the bright light of the microscope, the reddish tumor surface appeared imposingly large and close at the same time. I realized, though, that what met the eye was only the tip of the iceberg, with dangers lurking immediately behind the seemingly tranquil scene. The only way to stay out of trouble was to decrease the size of the tumor, which would give us the opportunity to see around the tumor and, thus, fastidiously protect the normal anatomy. I entered the tumor using the previously described ultrasound device that breaks down and aspirates the tumor tissue, confident that as long as I stayed inside the tumor, the surrounding neurovascular anatomy would be safe from an injury. Viewed under the microscope, the scene at this point was one of robust bleeding from the inner walls of the tumor, which obscured the field and required frequent hemostasis by applying bipolar electric current to the points of bleeding. It took some time before enough of the tumor tissue was removed for the upper pole of the tumor capsule to begin to collapse and recede from the surrounding anatomy. Focusing the microscope on that area, we could see the upper segment of the basilar artery and two of its important branches, known by the acronyms of PCA and SCA, covered by the thin and translucent arachnoid membrane. As the tumor capsule was further freed from the arachnoid, the brain stem came into view, recognizable by its glistening off-white appearance. Soon, proceeding down along the brain stem, we came upon the impressively splayed and thinned-out fifth cranial nerve, and again, it took some time to separate painstakingly each and every branch of that nerve from the tumor capsule. As more of the tumor tissue was removed from within the capsule, it became possible to free the inferior tumor pole from the facial and hearing nerves in the posterior fossa. Working alternately from the upper and lower tumor poles, we could finally free the capsule from all of its attachments to the arachnoid overlying the brain stem, the cranial nerves and vessels, and remove it completely.

It is difficult to put into words the incredible sight; I suppose words such as *majestic* and *serene* come to mind. There in the upper reaches of the exposure, the most fragile of them all, the fourth cranial nerve dangled freely, along with the PCA and SCA arteries. Directly in front of us, we were facing the ivory-colored brain stem pulsing with life, rising and ebbing gently with each respirator cycle and, thus, intermittently hiding the basilar artery trunk. By our focusing the microscope on the lower reaches of the exposure, the facial and hearing nerves and another artery, known as the AICA, wrapping around these nerves, came into view behind the translucent arachnoid membrane. With the pressure against the brain stem relieved, the brain fluid was now flowing unimpeded, bathing clean the brain stem and the cranial nerves from residual blood droplets.

N woke up in the recovery room with no neurological deficits save for a mild residual numbness in the right side of her face. The histological examination of the tissue confirmed the diagnosis of a grade I benign meningioma. A follow-up MRI showed no evidence of residual tumor tissue. The thrilling sensation that only neurosurgeons are privileged to experience following the successful conclusions of such difficult operations can be seductive indeed; it certainly helps to ameliorate the desolation of a failure. Looking back, it is difficult to say which of the two feelings lingers longer. I suspect the latter one does. In fact, it never quite fades away.

OF MARRIAGE AND FAMILY

All of us bring into our marriages the history and traditions of the families we grew up in. Neurosurgeons also bring into the marriage the passion for their arduous profession. Indeed, being overly consumed by our specialty, seduced by our successes, and aggrieved by our failures has caused some of my colleagues to fail in other aspects of life, family, and society. I am sure that I too could have done better as a husband and father. I am nevertheless happy to say that Anne and I are still having a thriving marriage. Anne remains my best friend and protector and the subject of my admiration, not only for her intellect and wisdom but also for her inexhaustible physical attractiveness. If anything, our spiritual rapport and intimate relationship matured and grew as we got older and had to overcome the infirmities of age and illness. Surely, aging is not synonymous with absence of passion. Yet it would be injudicious to say that intellectual and spiritual kinship and physical affinity are spontaneous and effortless gifts of life. We both had to work at our relationship and adjust, proactively at the beginning of our marriage and more spontaneously as time went by.

Anne is a voracious reader, and it was only natural that she joined a ladies' book club attached to her parish in Winnetka. Their preferred literature was books with spiritual themes not necessarily condoned by the church. I had to catch up by reading books of my interest so we could maintain an intellectual discourse. Reading sparked an interest in writing. I have been a steady contributor to the neurosurgical literature. Discoursing in writing on neurosurgical topics related to neuroscience or technical neurosurgery requires using sound investigative methods in a cogent, precise, and concise manner supported by statistical data and a pertinent review of the existing literature on the subject. Writing a literary essay allows a greater degree of latitude, for the message might simply be an opinion or argument by the author on a host of topics, not necessarily requiring an ironclad proof. In order to pursue my interests, I joined the Chicago Literary Club, where I presented several essays on different topics. Our intellectual commitments provided for a lively discussion at the dinner table.

Over the years, Anne and I shared similar views on social and political issues. Upon arriving in the United States, we embraced American patriotism and customs and did our best to bestow those sentiments on our children. We also shared same proclivities as to ambience and decorum, preferring subdued atmospheres and sedate elegance. We eschew loud and shrill conversations, preferring quiet and reasoned discourse. I was addicted to regular exercise, something Anne did not share in intensity. While traveling, though, we enjoyed walking for hours on end, surely more so than following the culinary trail. We also shared a lack of enthusiasm for attending musical performances, preferring instead to listen to music at home. Unfortunately, neither Anne nor I have a musical ear, which made us, in a way, musical pariahs among our friends, most of whom were erudite in matters of music and music history.

Looking back, it would appear that we had no contentious marital issues. Yet there were undercurrents that threatened to silently erode the cohesiveness of the family. One of these was the family's expression of faith. I was brought up in the Serbian Orthodox faith, and Anne grew up in the Catholic tradition. A casual observer could rightly say, "Why was that a problem? Both are Christian faiths based on similar trinity doctrines, with the difference being largely in the political structures and hierarchy of the two churches." Indeed, we did not want the centuries-old political issues between the two churches to intrude into our family, so staying true to our traditions, we celebrated both the Catholic holy days and, two weeks later, the Orthodox. Nevertheless, the dual message, as much as it was based on respect and tolerance, inevitably led to a less-than-firm sense of belonging, which I understand on an intellectual level but also regret emotionally; it was the result of a union of two cultures and two faiths common in this magnificent land of ours.

To consider a durable marriage solely as a work in progress would be wrong, for it would connote a perpetual struggle to maintain harmony. Rather, a successful marriage is a spiritual and physical amalgamation of two lives on a common path of shared milestones. To raise a family is not only a challenge but also a commitment toward a more promising future.

I was told by some who have read this memoir that it is predominantly centered on my professional life and is short on presenting my human face. This might be so for the simple reason that I have been immersed in my work 24–7. The stories of my patients, their trust in me, and their ultimate fates are my human face. For close to five decades, there has never been a hiatus in my life during which I would have cast away my profession and pursued a different interest or passion. It might also be true that in these memoirs, I have avoided uncovering the deepest recesses of my soul, for we all guard a precious intimacy with some of our feelings and memories, cherishing them for ourselves and remaining reluctant, for one reason or other, to share them even with those closest to us. There are also thoughts, impulses, and desires that we are aware of only dimly. They remain shrouded in obscurity yet contribute to our character and influence our actions.

Over the years, my friends and colleagues, some of whom regretted their choices in life, occasionally asked me if, given the chance to do it over again, I would have chosen the same path in my life. Clearly, my answer had to be in the affirmative, for the choice of any other career would have meant disowning my work, which I loved and had so much passion for. Surely, if I were disappointed in my life choices, this would have meant abandoning my patients, to whom I owe an immense gratitude, and worse yet, it would have meant denying my family. More than anything, it would have meant that my life was a vicarious existence without meaning or purpose.

THE VIRTUOSITY OF VESTIBULAR SCHWANNOMAS

One of the most challenging skull-base operations is the removal of a vestibular schwannoma, previously known as the acoustic neuroma. This is a benign tumor that originates from the sheath enveloping the vestibular nerves, which relate to balance. Even when the tumor is small, removing it can be a probing undertaking, as the tumor can adhere to the adjacent hearing and facial nerves. Considerable skills are required to separate the tumor from these cranial nerves without injury in order to avoid deafness and facial paralysis. A facial paralysis means that one side of the face sags, with the corner of the mouth drooping, resulting in drooling of the saliva. More importantly, a patient with a facial paralysis is unable to close the eye, which in turn can cause an injury to the cornea, leading to blindness. This is especially true if the patient simultaneously lost feeling in that eye due to a concurrent compression by the tumor of the fifth cranial nerve, the trigeminal nerve that is responsible for feeling in the face and the corneal sensation. A vestibular schwannoma is nestled in a rather confined space between the brain stem and cerebellum on one side and the inner ear bone on the other. A large vestibular schwannoma can

IVAN CIRIC, MD

severely distort and compress the brain stem, stretch the facial nerve to the point of unrecognition with the naked eye, and displace other cranial nerves, along with the essential arterial vessels. It is clear, therefore, that these structures would be in harm's way during an operation for removal of these tumors. An injury to the brain stem and to the adjacent cranial nerves can result in neurologic complications, such as unsteadiness, paralysis of extremities, and difficulty with swallowing (leading to bouts with pneumonia), or even be fatal; the larger the tumor, the greater the risks and the greater the need for extensive experience on the part of the surgeon. When it proceeds smoothly, though, the journey through the cascade of operative stages as observed under the operating microscope can be aesthetically pleasing.

To illustrate the challenges of such an operation, I shall tell the story of L, twenty years of age, whom I saw in urgent consultation after an MRI revealed the presence of a large tumor consistent in appearance and location with a vestibular schwannoma. A cascade of symptoms prompted the MRI. It all started with chronic buzzing and decreased hearing in her right ear when she was eighteen. For a while, these were her only symptoms. Then, some three weeks prior to seeing me, L became progressively unsteady. Shortly thereafter, she became aware of a loss of sensation in the right side of her face and in the left side of her body. This was followed by double vision. Two days prior to her visit with me, L developed severe headaches in conjunction with early morning vomiting. On examination, L appeared listless. The examination further revealed a swelling of the optic nerve heads, indicative of a significant increase in intracranial pressure, and a difficulty with outward motion of the right eye, which explained her double vision. The right side of her face and her right cornea had lost feeling. She also had abnormal, hyperactive reflexes in her left leg. In addition to the large tumor occupying practically the entire right posterior fossa, the MRI also showed an obstructive hydrocephalus. This finding explained L's headaches and lethargy. Clearly, we were faced with an emergency requiring prompt action to alleviate the increased pressure mounting inside the brain cavities and in the posterior fossa, threatening respiratory arrest.

I showed L and her mother the rather impressive MRI and CT scan findings and explained the need to alleviate urgently the raised intracranial pressure by relieving the hydrocephalus. To that end, we had two choices. The first one was to proceed with an external ventricular drainage, during which the accumulated cerebrospinal fluid would be drained in a controlled fashion on a temporary basis into a series of sterile containers. The second choice was to detour the accumulated brain fluid on a durable basis by inserting, underneath L's skin, a series of interconnected tubes and valves that would regulate cerebrospinal fluid outflow from the enlarged brain cavities into the abdominal cavity, a procedure also known as a shunt. I chose to recommend the shunt procedure for the simple reason that I was uncertain this unprecedented, large vestibular schwannoma could be removed to a sufficient degree to reestablish brain fluid flow through the normal anatomic channels. L's mother, clearly anguished with indecision, was initially reluctant to accept any notion of a surgical intervention and requested a second-opinion consultation, preferably from outside of Evanston Hospital. In my professional life, I have always been open to second-opinion consultations, sometimes recommending the consultant if the patient so desired and at other times letting the patient make the choice, with me facilitating such an encounter by making the necessary arrangements. In L's case, with the hydrocephalus threatening to cause a sudden, irreparable deterioration of the patient's condition or even be fatal, there was no time to bring in an outside consultant, which usually takes time to arrange. We agreed that I should secure a second opinion from my associate Dr. Joe Tarkington, which I was able to obtain within less than half an hour. Joe agreed with my assessment and recommended surgery to relieve the hydrocephalus. Finally, the mother and L consented.

The shunt procedure was carried out the same evening with excellent results: L woke up from the anesthetic much more alert than she had been on admission to the hospital, her headaches had vanished, and she no longer vomited. This initial success brought a smile to L's face and established the necessary trust between her mother and me.

Yet the arduous journey to ultimate healing had just begun. I recommended a few days of treatment with a brain steroid called dexamethasone, which reduces the swelling in the structures surrounding the tumor, including the cerebellum and the brain stem. Using this medication prior to surgery can protect swollen brain tissues prone to hemorrhage from surgical manipulations. Indeed, after five days of treatment with this medication, L's neurological state improved further in that the numbness in her face receded, and she became steadier on her feet.

The time had come to deal with the tumor itself. Again, I met with mother and daughter. L, much more lucid by now, participated cogently in our discussion. I explained the necessity of removing the tumor. The benign nature and the size of the tumor precluded other forms of treatment, such as radiation or chemotherapy. I explained the preparations for surgery, the anesthesia, and the sequence of the actual operative steps. During our discussion, I did my best to soften the impact of the mandatory informed consent on a fragile twenty-year-old soul by cushioning the information about the myriad possible complications with soothing words of encouragement and hope, for a positive mental attitude on the part of a patient facing imminent surgery is essential for a salutary outcome. I promised only one thing: I would dedicate every fiber of my being, both humanly and professionally, to the task. The necessary trust was established.

On the morning of surgery, everybody was upbeat and positive, with me and my team eager for the challenge. I also knew that I could always solicit advice from my associate Joe Tarkington if needed. I approached the tumor via a right posterior fossa craniotomy. Meanwhile, the anesthesiologist instituted measures that decreased the tension in the posterior fossa. Indeed, the dura over the right posterior fossa began to pulsate, indicating that the pressure within the compartment containing the tumor was under control. Upon opening the dura, we saw the swollen pale yellowish cerebellum, with its usually pronounced ridges flattened out. Off to the side, we saw the very back of the reddish-orange tumor capsule peeking out behind the cerebellum. We were aware that the controlled pressure situation within the posterior fossa, which contained the large tumor and the swollen cerebellum, was but a temporary truce that could suddenly blow up. Such a dreadful occurrence, usually related to an unexpected respiratory obstruction, can cause the cerebellum to protrude out of the skull and become strangulated in the craniotomy opening. With this in mind, our strategy was to swiftly open the tumor capsule and core out the tumor interior until a meaningful reduction in tumor size was accomplished, at which point it would become safer to start going around the tumor by collapsing the tumor capsule in search of the cranial nerves and the brain stem hidden behind the tumor. The cranial nerves most at risk were, in addition to the facial nerve, the ninth and tenth cranial nerves, which are responsible for the all-important swallowing mechanism. As for the hearing nerve, we knew that saving hearing on the right side would have been illusory. Therefore, without further delay, we opened the exposed tumor capsule and began removing the tumor tissue. At this point in the procedure, we were consoled by the knowledge that as long as we stayed within the confines of the tumor capsule, we were safe, with no possibility of injuring the surrounding neural and vascular structure. Of course, we had to be careful not to breech the tumor capsule from within the tumor—a dreadful prospect should it happen—as the tumor capsule abutted against the brain stem. Due to a rich blood supply to the tumor, there was conspicuous bleeding inside the tumor capsule each time a slab of tumor was removed, requiring frequent intermittent hemostasis that slowed our progress. We were into the seventh hour of the procedure by the time a meaningful internal decompression was accomplished, giving us the opportunity to go around the tumor capsule with the final goal of removing it. This is a much riskier part of the procedure when the neural elements, such as the cranial nerves, brain stem, and numerous important arteries and veins, are in harm's way. This proved to be relatively straightforward when it came to identifying and freeing the severely distorted fifth cranial nerve, which brings sensation to the face and eye (in the upper part of the posterior fossa), and the less-compressed ninth and tenth cranial nerves (below the tumor). With these cranial nerves freed and protected and with the arterial branches that supply blood to the brain stem also out of harm's way, we turned our attention to the most arduous and trying part of the operation: identifying and freeing the facial nerve, which, if injured, would cause a lifelong disfigurement of L's face. This is not a life-threatening injury but surely would be a life-changing one for this twenty-year-old beautiful young woman.

At this juncture, eleven hours into the operation, it became necessary to regroup and reassess the patient's condition and our stamina. Anesthetic-wise, the patient was medically stable with all parameters in the normal range. I felt pretty good, encouraged and emboldened to proceed, which I did after a pit stop and two glasses of orange juice. After we identified the facial nerve at the brain stem, it took another four hours of meticulous surgical maneuvers under high-power microscopic magnification to free the tissue-paper-thin facial nerve from the slack and redundant tumor capsule, all along stimulating the nerve cables, only to obtain a robust response from the facial EMG electrodes, signifying preserved function. As the redundant tumor capsule was gradually reduced in size, we finally came upon the whiteness of the severely indented brain stem. At the end of the operation, the last vestiges of the tumor were freed from the facial nerve within the facial nerve canal in the inner ear bone. Thus, the tumor was finally conquered after a lengthy battle in an incredibly complex field, during which time appeared to stand still only to intermittently change pace and fly by in a torrent of surgical maneuvers. We were basking in the wondrous beauty of restored human brain anatomy glowing under the microscope's brilliant light. In the depth of the cavernous-appearing right posterior fossa lurked the slender ivory-colored brain stem carrying the trunk of the fifth cranial nerve. Close to the partition between the two brain compartments was the vulnerable fourth cranial nerve, serving eye movements, and at the bottom of the operative site, the splayed-out cables of the ninth and tenth cranial nerves appeared sturdy and unscathed. In the middle of the tumor bed cavity, the intact, elongated, looping, and incredibly thin facial nerve was dangling between the point of its origin at the brain stem and the point where it enters the inner ear bone. The beauty of the final scene was enhanced by the pulsing of the brain stem, synchronous with the beat of the heart, signifying life and the promise of healing.

After reassuring ourselves that there was no residual bleeding in the tumor bed cavity, which had begun to fill gradually with the brain fluid, as the fluid was now free to flow along its restored anatomic channels, we closed the operative site layer by layer with greatest attention to detail. L woke up in the recovery room with not a shred of facial muscle weakness and with no other neurological deficits save for the loss of hearing in her right ear. The thrill and the rush of elation at having succeeded after a grueling eighteen-hour operation are not only soothing but also empowering. I returned home at dawn to the tune of chirping orioles announcing another glorious day.

In my subsequent career, I had five more vestibular schwannoma marathons. During one of those lengthy procedures, I suffered from exhaustion and had to be temporarily replaced by a team member. The remainder of the vestibular schwannomas I had the privilege of operating upon, most of them in collaboration with the neuro-otology team, were all smaller, so we were able to preserve not only the facial nerve function but also the hearing in some of the patients. Our technique and results of hearing preservation were published in the neurosurgical literature and received laudable peer review commentaries from experts in the field.

Recently, the number of patients with vestibular schwannomas requiring surgery has decreased. Surgeons are now reporting salutary results, especially in elderly patients, when treating smaller vestibular schwannomas with focused high-energy-beam radiation therapy. The indications for this treatment modality have gradually widened to encompass younger patients as well, although some controversy in this regard persists in light of the possible long-term side effects of radiation.

WHAT YOU SHOULD KNOW ABOUT HERNIATED DISCS, SPINAL STENOSIS, AND BACK PAIN

My interest in spinal surgery was triggered by my mentors, all of whom performed spinal surgery. The most common procedure I participated in was the operation for a herniated lumbar disc. Occasionally, they would perform laminectomy for spinal stenosis, and even more rarely, their patients underwent fusion operations in collaboration with orthopedic surgeons. These were elaborate undertakings requiring lengthy incisions. Looking back, it is my impression that the extended degree of spine exposure was necessary for the surgeon to visualize the pathology with both eyes. In time, I also became intrigued by a puzzling lack of precisely defined surgical indications in patients with herniated discs and spinal stenosis, a conundrum that frequently reflected adversely on the surgical outcomes.

Before I say a few words about spinal surgery, I should explain the basic makeup of the human spine in simple terms. Let me begin by comparing the human spine to a bony pipe. Instead of a single rigid, bony pipe that would preclude flexibility, the human spine is made out of bony rings (the vertebrae), which are stacked one on top of the other in a gentle curve. A single vertebra is similar in design to a Super Bowl ring in that it has a large diamond-like bone, also known as the vertebral body, and a relatively slender arch. Two adjacent vertebrae are coupled with joints positioned sideways and reinforced with tough bands called ligaments. Between the two adjacent vertebral bodies lies a disc shaped cartilage, the intervertebral disc, which acts like a cushion between the two vertebral bodies. Under normal anatomic circumstances, the disc does not protrude into the opening of the vertebral ring. At the top, the spine docks with the opening at the bottom of the skull, known as the foramen magnum. At the bottom, the spinal canal ends in the tailbone. The dura that wallpapers the inside of the skull continues down the spinal canal as a hose, usually referred to as the dural sac. It contains cerebrospinal fluid, the spinal cord, and spinal nerves. Between two adjacent vertebrae, a pair of spinal nerves, the nerve roots, exits the spine, one on either side, to contribute to the motor and sensory nerves that go to the extremities. As it leaves the spinal canal, a nerve root is surrounded by an extension of the dura, the nerve root sleeve. The sleeve attaches to the nerve root, preventing cerebrospinal fluid from leaking out.

A herniated disc means that a portion of the disc cartilage protrudes into the spinal canal. The protrusion can vary in scope and size, from a simple bulge to a sizable fragment that has broken off from the disc cartilage and migrated into the spinal canal. When this occurs in the cervical spinal canal, a herniated disc can compress the dura sac containing the spinal cord, threatening the function of all four extremities. In the lumbar spine, which is more capacious, a herniated disc usually affects one of the nerve roots, causing leg pain, also described as sciatica. When the pressure on a nerve root is pronounced or prolonged, it can cause muscle weakness in one or (rarely) both lower extremities, loss of sensation, and even bladder paralysis. It is important to listen carefully to the patient's history since precisely defined symptoms can help differentiate a herniated disc from other types of spinal pathology. Typically, the sciatic pain caused by a herniated lumbar disc is made worse by sitting, while it is relieved by standing up or lying down. It is also important to perform a thorough neurologic examination, since the findings can give a clue as to which of the multiple discs in the lumbar or cervical spine might have herniated. For example, in a patient with sciatic pain, the finding of a foot drop is consistent with a disc herniation between the fourth and fifth lumbar vertebrae. More ominously, the finding of decreased sensation in the crotch should alert the neurosurgeon to the likelihood of a large herniation requiring immediate imaging with MRI and prompt surgical attention. In the case of a cervical disc herniation, arm pain radiating toward the thumb side of the hand is consistent with a herniated disc between the fifth and sixth cervical vertebrae. Similarly, the finding of a weakness in the triceps is suggestive of a herniation between the sixth and seventh cervical vertebrae, and so on. The permutations of possible symptoms and neurologic findings in patients suffering from herniated discs are manifold and require a considerable acumen of knowledge and experience to be interpreted correctly. A lack of clinical expertise invites the danger of misinterpreting the imaging findings, which, when taken out of context of the clinical information and findings, can be confusing. This is especially true with the elderly, in whom the imaging signs of wear and tear usually affect multiple spinal levels without necessarily being symptomatic.

The indications for operating on a herniated lumbar or cervical disc have varied widely among neurosurgeons and still do so. This prompted me to define my own indications. In patients with a lumbar or cervical disc herniation, surgery is indicated if the examination shows evidence of a significant neurologic deficit, be it evidence of a pronounced muscle weakness or loss of sensation, especially if it is increasing in scope. Moreover, surgery should also be considered when the imaging studies show a sizable herniation that, in the neurosurgeon's estimation, clearly threatens neurologic functions. Finally, an intractable arm or leg pain that fails to respond to exhaustive conservative therapy and is caused by a clearly defined herniated disc in an appropriate anatomic location can also be considered an indication for surgery.

The basic premise of an operation for a herniated lumbar disc is to retrieve the herniation from the spinal canal and thereby relieve the pressure on the nerve root without causing an injury. During my residency, the patients undergoing surgery for lumbar or cervical disc herniation remained hospitalized anywhere from five to seven days after surgery. The prolonged convalescence was in part secondary to a tardy healing caused by the large incisions and extensive muscle and bone dissections. Prompted early in my career by a serious neurologic complication in one of my patients, in whom it was difficult to discern with the naked eye the true extent of a sprawling herniation, I decided to apply my experience with the use of the operating microscope in cranial surgery to operations for removal of lumbar and cervical disc herniation. The introduction of

IVAN CIRIC, MD

microsurgical techniques in spinal surgery has greatly reduced operative complications, especially the incidence of injuries to the dural sac and nerve roots, which can cause neurologic disability and leakage of the cerebrospinal fluid. By the mid-1990s, operations for removal of herniated discs were performed nationwide on an outpatient basis through minimally invasive entry ports. Currently, the operation for a herniated lumbar disc, colloquially known as a microdiscectomy, is a straightforward task, albeit not without pitfalls. For example, since the operation is performed with the patient lying prone, pressure on the dependent eye can result in blindness. It is also important to precisely localize the desired level of the herniated cervical or lumbar disc to avoid proceeding with surgery at a wrong level—unfortunately, not an unheard-of occurrence. This is best accomplished with appropriate intraoperative imaging that under certain circumstances, such as obesity, might be difficult to interpret. It is advisable, therefore, that the imaging be interpreted for accuracy by both the surgical team and the radiologist. The operation is performed through an inch-long skin incision, using specially designed entry ports. The spinal canal is entered through a small opening made by drilling away part of the two adjacent vertebral arches. A great deal of concentration and caution is required in order not to breach the dura sac and injure the underlying nerve root. There are instances when the whitish herniated disc stands out against the dura sac and is easily removed. There are also instances, however, when the herniation is tucked deeply and tightly under the dura sac or the nerve root. A considerable operative deftness is required to extract the herniation without causing injury in such cases. The end point of the operation usually declares itself when the dura sac and the nerve root become relaxed. Any evidence of residual tightness or resistance observed in the dura sac and the nerve root usually means that there is still a residual herniated disc fragment present, which must be found and removed, lest the patient wakes up after surgery with the same pain. Given that the herniation was removed completely and no injury occurred in the process, the patient will wake up relieved of pain and ready to be discharged a few hours later. It is not an exaggeration to say that properly executed microdiscectomies have relieved the suffering and brought smiles to the faces of hundreds of thousands of patients. I attest to that not only since I have operated myself on countless patients but also since my wife, Anne, was relieved of agonizing pain after undergoing a microdiscectomy in the late 1980s by noted Pittsburgh neurosurgeon Dr. Joseph Maroon, a pioneer of lumbar microdiscectomies. However, it is also true that a lumbar microdiscectomy can permanently alter for worse the quality of life in a patient in whom untoward surgical manipulations caused an injury to the spinal cord or a nerve root, resulting either in a disabling neurological deficit or in a permanent and just-as-agonizing burning pain. Consequently, even though surgery for removal of a herniated disc does not have the same implications as a brain operation, it is nevertheless incumbent on neurosurgeons to approach it with the same degree of commitment to excellence.

Spinal stenosis is a condition that usually afflicts lumbar spines of older individuals. The basic feature of spinal stenosis is a narrowing of the spinal channel due to a thickening of bony, joint, and ligament structures of the vertebrae, which encroach upon the dura sac. In the majority of patients, this thickening occurs as a consequence of the aging process, which might be superimposed on a congenitally slender spinal canal. As a result of the narrowing of the spinal canal, the dura sac and the nerve elements in it gradually become compressed, leading to symptoms such as leg pain, which, in contrast to the sciatic pain caused by a herniated disc, is characteristically provoked and aggravated by standing and walking and relieved by sitting or lying down. Even bending the torso forward alleviates the pain. It is not surprising, therefore, that patients with spinal stenosis prefer to lean on objects, such as the kitchen counter or a shopping cart. In its latter stages, spinal stenosis can result in weakness and a loss of sensation in the legs. Patients with spinal stenosis might also complain of back pain, although there is some debate as to the origin of the back pain. To my thinking, a symptomatic lumbar spinal stenosis as a pathologic entity implies a compression of the neural elements in the lumbar spine that is manifested in leg pain and not back pain. The back pain is in fact caused by the wear and tear of aging—by the arthritic changes in the intervertebral discs and in the joints that couple two adjacent vertebrae. The operative procedure, a laminectomy, is designed to open the spine and relieve the pressure on the dural sac and the nerve elements within it. This accomplishes relief from leg pain only and does nothing for the back pain. The laminectomy should not interfere with the spinal joints so as not to cause the spine to become unstable, which in itself could cause back pain. In order to prevent this from occurring, in some instances, a stabilization of the spinal column, a procedure called a fusion, becomes necessary. There is still no uniform opinion among spinal surgeons as to the precise indications for a fusion. To my thinking, a fusion is more likely to be indicated in younger individuals with spinal stenosis who present with predominantly lower back pain and who have imaging evidence of instability in the lumbar spine. The recent advances in minimally invasive spinal techniques and in spinal instrumentation have made the fusion procedure simpler and safer.

IN THE OPERATING ROOM ON SEPTEMBER 11, 2001

My patient was a cantankerous seventy-three-year-old man with spinal stenosis. After failed conservative therapy, he was scheduled for laminectomy on September 11, 2001. I woke up that day with a foreboding feeling, because in spite of all the efforts to put him at ease through numerous presurgical meetings and explanations, my patient's trust in my abilities was porous at best. After obtaining several additional consultations, he decided to have the operation performed by me after all.

It was my judgment that my patient did not require a fusion. He had no instability in his spine. His spinal stenosis involved three vertebrae, requiring a three-level laminectomy. I was confident that relieving his spinal stenosis would free him of his leg pain and improve the numbness and weakness in his legs, although to what extent I could not foresee, since it is difficult to know ahead of surgery how much of the nerve damage is permanent and how much is temporary. I was also concerned that his lower back pain would not improve, since the operation addresses only the relief of pressure on the spinal nerves and, thus, the leg symptoms only. I did my best to explain this to my patient, but in spite of repeated conversations, I was not sure I was able to make him feel comfortable. Therefore, we were both uncomfortable. In the holding area, I greeted my patient, who was on a gurney. I placed my hand on his shoulder and gently asked if he would turn around so I could mark the area on his back, as required by the hospital protocol. He retorted brusquely, "Don't you know where to operate? Have you reviewed my record? By the way, I don't want this flunky of yours to touch me during surgery," and he pointed to the senior resident, a smart and skillful young man. I reassured him that my plan was still the same as per our previous discussions, and I also explained the important role played by the resident during surgery. It was actually painful to ask him to sign the consent. In order to bring some humor to the situation, I told him that if I owned the joint, he would not have to sign, but since I just worked there, the rules and regulations required us each to pen down our yours truly. In the operating room, he asked the anesthesiologist, "Is this your first anesthetic?" The graying anesthesiologist responded calmly, "No, second."

With the patient anesthetized, we turned him prone, stomach down on the operating table with the chest and abdomen supported by a special frame, and we took care to protect his dependent eye and peripheral nerves from any pressure points. The back was prepared and draped in the usual sterile fashion, and the area to be operated upon was localized with appropriate imaging. A midline incision was made overlying the three involved vertebrae. The good man had a three-inch fat layer we had to go through before reaching the muscles covering the spinal arches. Bleeding points were controlled meticulously with low-level electric current delivered precisely with a special forceps. The muscles were then freed from their attachment to the spinal arches. A second, positive radiological confirmation of the spinal levels was obtained, and the arches were removed utilizing a specially designed high-speed drill under the operating microscope.

During the work under the operating microscope, as I was drilling away the last bits of the bony spurs over the exiting nerve roots, the scrub nurse, after conferring in hushed tones with the circulating nurse, announced, "Dr. Ciric, I just heard that New York and Washington were bombed." Considering that using a drill in the vicinity of the precious nerve roots requires utmost concentration in order to prevent injury, I stopped what I was doing and, looking up incredulously from the microscope, responded, "Yes, and I am the president of the United States," before continuing with my work to completion.

In the recovery room, I asked, "How is the old pain?"

"Just from the incision, Doc, the old pain is gone, but are you sure you did not operate on the wrong level?" retorted my doubtful Thomas. I reassured him that everything was okay and that there was no nerve damage, but I knew I would have my hands full in the ensuing follow-up of a determinedly unhappy albeit pain-free patient. Meanwhile, the tragedy of 9/11 unfolded in front of my resident's and my eyes as we entered the lounge and witnessed the carnage on the screen of the TV set. The first thought that came to me was *Who are these evil savages, and how were they able to commit such an atrocity against unsuspecting, innocent people on a balmy, clear, sunny, beautiful September day?* Soon the dark, billowing smoke emanating from the World Trade Center's towers replaced the blue skies. Down on the street, there was mayhem, with people running away from the damaged towers through a cloud of dust and smoke that spread rapidly like a dusty avalanche. Then I remembered that my three children lived in the city.

I called my wife, and she told me with great relief that she had heard from our eldest daughter and from our son but not from our second daughter, who, it turns out, was stuck in traffic on the George Washington Bridge. After seeing to it that my patient was doing well and after making rounds, during which I offered encouragement to my patients, I returned home, sad and angry at the same time. I was deeply saddened that so many innocent lives had been lost and furious at the perpetrators who'd dared to violate our country, hurt our people, and infringe on our freedom. September 11, 2001, will remain permanently etched in my soul. It also awakened the long-suppressed but not extinguished memories of suffering and loss of life I witnessed in my youth.

IVAN CIRIC, MD

THE WEEKEND SPOILED—OR WAS IT?

There is some magic to Friday afternoons, when physicians are eagerly getting ready for a well-deserved weekend of rest and recreation. Unfortunately, it is also on Friday, usually in the late afternoon, when neurosurgeons are frequently called upon with an air of utmost urgency about a patient in need of immediate neurosurgical care. The exasperating thing about such a call is that the referring physician likely saw the patient three to four days earlier. Similarly, a CT or MRI might not have been interpreted until Friday afternoon. This lack of anticipatory timing on the part of the physicians who are not neurosurgeons can be frustrating, not only because it interferes with the neurosurgeon's weekend plans but also, more importantly, because the neurosurgeon frequently has to proceed with emergency surgery on the weekend, when the operational readiness of the surgical suite slows down. Sure, the neurosurgeon can refer the patient to a colleague on call for urgent cases over the weekend—but at the risk of offending the referring physician, who might feel slighted and hence never refer another patient in the future. It was on precisely such a late Friday afternoon when my beeper went off with the message to call back a respected neurologist and personal friend. I was surprised when I heard him say, "Ivan, I have here in my office a young man with a rapidly progressive myelopathy who needs to be seen by a neurosurgeon today." As it turned out, the referring neurologist initially saw the patient on Tuesday, the MRI was not obtained till Thursday afternoon and not interpreted until Friday afternoon. Be that as it may, I scrapped whatever plans I had for that evening and arranged to see the patient immediately. When I entered the curtained-off room in the emergency department, I was greeted by a tall gentleman in his late thirties and his wife, both anxious but not doubting that I could be of help. It turns out that the patient was the brother-in-law of a physician on the staff who knew my reputation and recommended me to the patient.

The patient told the following story. About a week to ten days prior, while in the gym lifting weights, he felt a sudden "pop" in his neck in conjunction with an electric-shock-like sensation radiating down his torso, arms, and legs. For a moment, his knees also buckled. He stopped with his workout and went home, feeling somewhat unsteady. The following morning, he got up only to be even more unsteady on his feet. He also began to experience numbness and tingling, predominantly toward the pinky side of his hands. In the ensuing days, he also became aware that every time he extended his neck to look up, he would experience the electric-shock-like sensations through his torso and extremities. Listening to the patient's history, I concluded that the most likely explanation for his symptoms was a sizable cervical disc herniation. On examination of this grossly unsteady man, I found signs consistent with cervical spinal cord compression. He had weakness and twitching in his left triceps. His tendon reflexes were increased, and he exhibited some abnormal reflexes, predominantly in his left hand and leg. The sensory examination revealed decreased pinprick perception on the right side below his collarbone. Finally, I was able to reproduce the electric-shock sensations by asking him to raise his chin. The sum clinical impression was that this gentleman suffered a cervical disc herniation with cord compression at approximately the sixth cervical vertebra level. The MRI confirmed the clinical impression. There was a large herniated disc compressing the spinal cord to less than half of its normal diameter. The spinal cord also showed evidence of swelling.

Clearly, we were dealing with a neurosurgical emergency requiring immediate intervention in order to prevent further and potentially irretrievable neurologic disability. The operation is done through an inch-long horizontal skin incision, usually on the right side of the neck, along a natural skin fold in order to minimize scar formation. While protecting the carotid artery and the jugular vein on one side of the exposure and the voice box and esophagus on the other, the surgeon reaches the spine in no time. During this part of the procedure, the voice box nerve is prone to injury, in which case the patient can wake up from the anesthetic permanently hoarse. The desired disc is identified with appropriate imaging and removed completely. The herniation thus becomes accessible in the depth of the space between the two vertebrae. Use of the operating microscope assures that the removal of the herniated disc fragments is executed with precision and safely. The gap between the two adjacent vertebral bodies is bridged over either by using a commercially available bone graft that is reinforced with a small plate or, more recently, by inserting and anchoring an artificial disc. In this case, I used the former technique, which eventually resulted in a solid bony union between the two vertebrae. The operation proceeded smoothly. Already in the recovery room, the patient noticed less tingling and improved dexterity in his hands. The subsequent course was salutary with complete neurologic recovery except for some lingering numbness in his torso, which is not surprising, considering the well-known fact that motor functions tend to recover ahead of sensory deficits.

I chose to describe this patient's case to emphasize how important it is to listen carefully to the patient's history, perform a thorough neurologic examination, and obtain and interpret the imaging studies without delay, all in order to maximize the likelihood of a good outcome.

THE TWO-FACED QUANDARY OF SPINAL TUMORS

There is nothing secretive about the designation of spinal tumors. As their name implies, they affect the spinal column and its contents. Cancerous spinal tumors are predominantly related to a primary cancer source elsewhere in the body that has spread to the spine. Almost every cancer can spread via the bloodstream to the spine. The cancerous tumors that frequently metastasize to the spine are breast, prostate, and kidney cancer. Lung cancer can also spread to the spine through direct invasion from the chest cavity. Metastatic tumors rarely, if ever, penetrate the dura and, thus, remain outside the dura sac. They also destabilize the spine as the soft tissues of the cancer replace the bony structures of the vertebrae. The main initial symptom of a metastatic tumor is neck or back pain, depending on the location of the tumor. Typically, the pain is usually worse at night, when the patient is recumbent. This important historical detail distinguishes cancer-related pain from back pain related to a herniated disc or spinal stenosis. As already mentioned, the pain secondary to a herniated disc is aggravated when the patient sits down or by neck movements if the herniation is in the cervical spine. Patients with spinal stenosis have more pain when they stand or walk. It is reasonable to say, therefore, that a persistent neck or back pain, especially if worse when the patient lies down at night, in a patient with a history of cancer should be considered as being secondary to a spinal metastasis until proven otherwise. Depending on the location of the spinal metastases, patients can also complain of arm pain if the tumor is in the cervical spine or leg pain if it involves the lower back. If the tumor involves the chest part of the spine, the pain might feel like a vice surrounding the chest cage. In a relatively short period, the patient can go on to develop a loss of strength and sensation in the arms, legs, or both. When this occurs, it constitutes a neurosurgical emergency. The treatment can be with chemo or radiation therapy in the early stages of the disease or with surgery if there is a need to relieve the pressure on the spinal cord and nerve roots or to stabilize the spine. Surgery for removal of a spinal metastasis can be a bloody proposition, associated with considerable blood loss, especially if the metastasis is from a kidney or thyroid cancer. The prognosis depends on the timeliness of the diagnosis and on the patient's condition relative to the primary cancer source.

Benign spinal tumors are less frequent than the metastatic tumors of the spine. The three most common benign spinal tumors are meningiomas, neurofibromas, and ependymomas. Neurofibromas originate from one of the spinal nerves, usually from a sensory branch. Ependymomas arise from the ependyma cells that line a tiny central canal that runs through the spinal cord. In contrast to the metastatic tumors, which are predominantly *outside* the dura sac, benign tumors are overwhelmingly *inside* the dura sac. The symptoms of benign spinal tumors are similar to those stemming from spinal metastases, although their onset is more insidious, and their progression more gradual. Since there is usually no history of cancer elsewhere in the body, a history of neck, arm, lower back, or leg pain is often at first erroneously interpreted as being due to arthritic changes or a herniated disc. A carefully taken history of an insidious onset of arm or leg pain that progresses gradually but also unrelentingly, especially if the pain is worse when the patient retires to bed at night, should alert an astute neurosurgeon to the possibility of a benign spinal tumor. Similarly, a thorough neurologic examination will reveal the location of the tumor even before imaging studies are obtained. While surgery for spinal metastases is by and large palliative, meaning that it is designed to ameliorate the symptoms and prevent neurologic deficits in patients who might be riddled with cancer, surgery for benign spinal tumors is not only curative but also a delightful—albeit challenging—exercise of surgical virtuosity and prowess. Neurosurgeons approach the former with reluctance and the latter with greatest enthusiasm. Two patients with benign spinal tumors, T and C, come to mind.

T was a fifty-seven-year-old graphic artist who first noticed pain in his right shoulder some eight months prior to seeing me. The pain grew gradually worse and prevented him from sleeping at night. An orthopedic surgeon who evaluated him first could not find anything wrong with the shoulder. Several months later, he became aware of a twitching in his right shoulder muscles. T became seriously concerned when he noted that he had started to drag his right leg. He consulted with a neurologist, who referred him to me. T, who was a little on the heavy size, as was his wife, greeted me jovially. "Hey, Doc, I hear we are both from the same neck of the woods," he chirped. "When did you leave the old country?" He added, "Isn't the Riesling from our area something else? Maybe I should down a flask of that nectar and cure myself." After we reminisced about our backgrounds and wine, he settled down, and I was able to examine him. The findings I elicited were fascinating and telling at the same time. The neurologic examination showed weakness and wasting of his right shoulder muscles, along with evidence of what is usually referred to as spasticity in his right leg, which he dragged slightly, similar to a patient who had suffered a stroke. I also found that he had no feeling of pain and temperature sensations in his left leg and torso up to his collarbone. When I told him of that finding, he exclaimed, "Well, I'll be darned! This explains why I nearly scalded my left foot when stepping into the bathtub the other day, only to realize that the water was hot after I placed my right foot into the tub."

To those discerning in the anatomy of the spinal cord, these findings, cumulatively known under the eponym Brown-Sequard syndrome, indicate pressure against the right side of the spinal cord from an extrinsic source in the cervical spine at approximately the fourth or fifth cervical vertebra. An MRI of the cervical spine confirmed the clinical impression; it showed an inch-and-a-half-large intradural tumor at the fifth cervical vertebra level, compressing the spinal cord from the right side to a sliver of its usual diameter. The MRI appearance of the tumor was consistent with a benign neurofibroma.

After we sat down and reminisced further about the old country, as T called it, I explained to T and his wife the need to remove his tumor in order to prevent him from becoming paralyzed. In the repertoire of my discussions with patients, it has always been my practice to back up ominous pronouncements with a cogent explanation as to the reasoning behind such an adverse prognosis. Thus, I told T and his wife that the spinal cord tolerates gradually increasing pressure by an extrinsic force for a while but only to a certain point. I reviewed the MRI with them, emphasizing the degree of compression. Judging by T's neurological deficit, which had accelerated in recent days, and in view of the MRI findings, which showed the spinal cord severely compressed and attenuated, I explained that the point at which the spinal cord would not tolerate any further increase in pressure against it, when the neurologic functions would swiftly and irretrievably decompensate, was not far off. A clear thinker, T logically asked, "And why would that be so, Doc? What really happens at that point?" In response, I explained that as the pressure against the spinal cord gradually increases at one point, the tiny arteries that provide blood supply to the cord also become compressed, resulting in a lack of blood supply to the cord—in essence, resulting in a spinal cord stroke with irreversible deleterious neurologic consequences. This explanation satisfied T, who then asked, "When can you do it, Doc?" After explaining the fundamental steps of the operation, I scheduled the surgery for the following day. T was otherwise a healthy individual, and he got the green light from his internist for me to proceed with surgery.

The essential concept of such an operation is to avoid placing any pressure against the spinal cord in the process of tumor removal, as any additional pressure could result in serious and possibly irreversible neurologic deficit. During the operation, we approached the tumor by removing the fifth cervical vertebra arch and part of the fourth arch, more so on the right side. Working under the operating microscope, I opened the dura in the midline, leaving the underlying arachnoid intact for the time being. The reddish-gray tumor became immediately visible through the translucent arachnoid. The opening of the arachnoid could prove tricky, as the release of the spinal fluid from the subarachnoid space can alter the pressure dynamics and cause more pressure against the spinal cord. Fortunately, the electrophysiological recordings conducted during the operation remained stable. After incising the tumor capsule, we removed the interior of the tumor using an ultrasonic aspirator armed with a precision tip. This maneuver resulted in an immediate slackening of the tumor capsule, which receded spontaneously from the spinal cord. The bleeding points within the tumor were treated with an application of low-grade bipolar current to prevent any spillage of blood around the spinal cord, which, if it were to occur, could not only obscure the operative field but also lead to painful scar formation down the road. Having decompressed the tumor from within, I was able to free the tumor capsule from the spinal cord. Yet the tumor remained tethered to the sensory nerve rootlets from which it originated. We divided these rootlets above and below the tumor making it possible to remove the tumor without placing even the slightest pressure against the spinal cord. The view of the attenuated cord pulsing with life and bathed in the water-clear spinal fluid, with not a drop of blood in it, is always astonishingly pleasing to the eye. The dura was stitched together, and the closure was reinforced with a sealant to prevent spinal fluid leakage. The surgical wound was closed in layers, with attention to detail in order to prevent postoperative complications such as a hematoma formation and infection. The frozen sections of the tumor specimen confirmed a neurofibroma.

T did beautifully after surgery, with many of the preoperative neurologic deficits gradually receding. At one year postoperatively, the only neurologic deficit remaining was a slightly decreased pain sensation in the left side of his body, below the nipple. He returned to full employment.

The case of C was different in that her tumor, an ependymoma, was inside the cervical spinal cord. C was a seventeen-year-old high school senior who presented with a six-month-long history of progressive unsteadiness and weakness in her hands, greater on the right side. She also admitted to some numbness in her shoulders but denied any bladder difficulties. On examination, C was unsteady on her feet. She had a marked weakness in her hands. By contrast, she had no weakness in her feet. The tendon reflexes in her legs were hyperactive, and she had abnormal reflexes consistent with spasticity. The sensory examination was interesting in that it revealed a loss of pain and temperature sensation over her shoulders, in a distribution mimicking a fashionable woman's cape, and reaching down into her hands. Interpreted anatomically, the neurological examination was consistent with a lesion situated inside the cervical spinal cord. The MRI confirmed the presence of a tumor within the cervical spinal cord, extending from the fourth to the sixth cervical vertebra. This segment of the spinal cord was significantly expanded by the oblong tumor within it. Compared to T's tumor, which was outside the spinal cord, to remove a tumor *inside* the spinal cord is much more challenging, as it requires splitting the cord in order to reach the tumor. Splitting the cord can be associated with a number of untoward neurologic consequences. I discussed the need to remove the tumor with C and her parents. In doing so, I did not diminish the potential dangers of the operation. The risks of surgery are also directly related to the preoperative neurologic functions. Specifically, the risks of surgery are fewest in a patient who prior to surgery has minimal neurologic deficit. In contrast, in a patient with advanced preoperative neurologic deficit, when the patient is already on the brink of becoming paralyzed, the likelihood that surgery would tip the scale in a harmful direction and that the patient would be worse off after surgery grows exponentially.

On the morning of surgery, I greeted C and her parents in the holding area of the surgical suite. Her mother held my hands and prayed before she pressed into my hands the likeness of Mary. For a brief moment, I felt overwhelmed with self-doubt. *Am I really ready to breach the anatomic integrity of this young woman's spinal cord, no matter how justified medically?* Then, as usually happens, the reset button in my brain swiftly switched the channels to the professionalism of the logic behind the need to remove the tumor.

In the operating room, C was anesthetized and equipped with a host of electrophysiological monitors for continuous observance of her spinal cord and nerve functions. The tumor was approached through a midline incision in the back of the neck. With the operating microscope in position, I opened the taut dura and subsequently the arachnoid membrane in the midline. Inspection of the spinal cord under the microscope revealed bluish discoloration underneath the groove that runs longitudinally along the line spanning the points of entry of the sensory nerve roots into the cord. Clearly, the tumor had thinned out and stretched apart the spinal cord fiber tracts in this area. This finding prompted me to suggest to my assistant,

IVAN CIRIC, MD

the senior resident on the service, that we should approach the tumor by splitting the cord along the thinned-out groove rather than in the midline, where, in my experience, the danger of the patient becoming more unsteady postoperatively was much greater. Since the tumor was approximately two inches in length, an incision into the cord of half that length would give us enough of a corridor to visualize the upper and lower poles of the tumor. Using the tiniest albeit sharpest knives and appropriate microseparators, we cautiously searched for and followed the natural cleavage planes between the spinal cord tracts. The operating microscope proved invaluable in this regard. This maneuver exposed the bluish-brown tumor surface. In keeping with the principle of first making a large tumor smaller, the tumor was entered and its contents removed. The tumor was soft, almost like wet pulp, and contained small pockets of blood clots here and there, which were gently removed. The tumor capsule was not as clearly defined as in T's case. Nevertheless, we were able to gently peel it off piecemeal from the surrounding spinal cord fiber tracts. Here and there, small remnants of the capsule were intimately attached to the fiber tracts and, in order to prevent injury, had to be left behind. During the procedure, the recordings from the electrophysiological monitoring remained stable, with only intermittent evidence of abnormal waves that would alert us to stop with tumor removal for a few moments until the recordings recovered to baseline. The closure of the wound proceeded in layers: dura, cervical muscles, subcutaneous layer, and skin. The histological examination of the tissue specimen revealed a low-grade ependymoma.

Postoperatively, C was temporarily more unsteady and required physical therapy. Within three months of surgery, she regained many of her lost neurologic functions. Six months after surgery, she walked with a barely noticeable degree of unsteadiness, and at one year, she resumed jogging. The only permanent deficit was the cape-like loss of pain and temperature sensation, because of which she had to be careful when going under a shower. C was followed for eight years with no evidence of a recurrence. The last time I saw her in follow-up before she moved to another state, I gave her the likeness of Mary that her mother, who in the meantime had passed away from cancer, had given me before surgery. I was rewarded with a long hug as she wept on my shoulder.

US HEALTH CARE: A CALLING OR AN INDUSTRY?

When I started practicing neurosurgery in 1967, the relationship between the physician and the patient, between the healer and the sick, was a very personal one. Except for the budding health insurance industry, there were no outside agents interceding between the two, especially not in an adversarial capacity. Shortly thereafter, the legal profession began to intrude by looking over physicians' shoulders under the premise of protecting the patients' welfare and interests. This was followed by a succession of additional constraining influences, such as the ever-tighter insurance industry purse and governmental regulations. The decreasing reimbursements by the insurance industry made maintaining a private practice increasingly more difficult, as the expenses began to exceed the revenues. The governmental regulations were brought on the heels of the ever-increasing health-care costs in need of curbing and with the aim of improving the overall quality of care. Unfortunately, they failed on the former score and partially on the second, as the regulations were designed to reward quantity of care, rather than quality, by establishing quantity benchmarks for hospitals (ICD 9) and physicians' reimbursement

(RVU). The recently enacted Affordable Care Act has provisions to rectify this in favor of quality of care. However, the strategy to accomplish this by establishing another governmental agency (Independent Payment Advisory Board) charged to define quality benchmarks remains controversial, especially with the medical profession. The governmental regulations and the Affordable Care Act prompted health-care providers to institute their own initiatives with the goal of eliminating errors and improving efficiency of health-care delivery. The cumulative effect of these changes has forced many physicians to either abandon the profession through early retirement or align their practices with health-care delivery organizations through a variety of relationships, from being straight salaried to a wide range of negotiated contracts. Straddled with high malpractice premiums in some of the medicolegally more volatile parts of the country, neurosurgeons had to adapt to the new paradigms of practicing their specialty. Nevertheless, neurosurgeons have remained faithful to the ethos of their profession, a calling and certainly not an industry.

To be sure, many of the changes instituted have in fact helped advance the cause of quality care. One could argue, for instance, that the intercession by the law profession might have protected patients from less than competent physicians. An example of a positive institutional change affecting quality of care was the conversion of paper-based health-care documentation to digital records. This has been a quantum leap forward in safeguarding human life, as it facilitated sharing of information among the multitude of physicians caring for a patient. At the same time, however, the computer became another agent sitting between the physician and the patient, detracting once again from the interpersonal relationship between the two. In addition, the digitally stored information has opened a Pandora's Box of infringed privacy requiring a new set of complex regulations and technology-based protective mechanisms. Another institutional novelty has been the establishment of a new bureaucracy under the genteel name of human resources, which among other responsibilities also regulates human behavior in the work place. For example, the explicit language uttered in the heat of an operation by some of the more domineering surgeons of yesteryear is no longer acceptable.

My personal viewpoint, reflecting the credo of the medical profession, rooted in the Hippocratic ethos and steeped in science, is that health care is a right and not a privilege and that medicine is based on humanism and not on business or politics. In short, I do believe that Americans are entitled to affordable health care. I doubt that many would argue with this statement. Without going into criticism or praise of the recently enacted Affordable Care Act (as codified by the US Supreme Court), let me just say that the devil is in the details as to financing this gargantuan program in the face of ever-escalating US health-care costs. The total cost of US health care in 2011 was a remarkable $2.6 trillion, or 17 percent of the US gross domestic product (GDP), a sum that is greater than the $2.3 trillion collected in tax revenues that year. Until the early 1980s, the US health-care cost was progressing along a mildly increasing curve parallel to Western European countries and other industrialized nations. Since the 1980s, the US health-care cost has taken off along a steeply inclined curve that is out of proportion to other industrialized nations. These data show that should the US health-care cost continue to escalate at the same rate, on the average of 6 percent per year with the GDP rising at 3 percent per year, the US health-care cost would consume 100 percent of the GDP by 2070. Theoretically, at that point, no resources would be left for the Social Security pension plan, national defense, infrastructure, education, or the judiciary system, to name but a few of the essential institutions in the existence of a country. The gravity of such a scenario is self-evident. Among the possible causes contributing to the ever-escalating cost of US health care, over-utilization of care stands out as the potentially greatest culprit. While there are numerous examples of health-care overutilization, one that is most frequently quoted (though not necessarily the most expensive one) is the disproportionately large number of magnetic resonance units (MRIs) in the United States compared to other industrialized nations. One might be also justified in asking if the increase in the number of older people—who are more disease prone—has contributed to the escalation of US health-care costs. Without entering into a discourse on the ethics of life and death, for this is not the purpose of these memoirs, I will say that there is ample evidence of an inappropriate allocation of health-care resources at the end of life, especially in the last six months of life. Such unconditional support of life under any and all circumstances, regardless of the patient's age or the insurmountable ravages of the disease, oftentimes has the unintended consequence of forsaking the dignity of life for the sake of life with no dignity.

Another contributor to the escalating cost of US health care is the medical liability system. In order to avoid lawsuits, physicians and surgeons tend to practice defensive medicine. One of the consequences of such defensive medical practice is

IVAN CIRIC, MD

that physicians often focus on proving what the patient is *not* suffering from or afflicted with rather than following the clues given by history and examination and targeting laboratory and imaging evaluation accordingly. The overall result is superfluous, extensive, and expensive testing for the sake of physician protection.

The present paradigm of US health-care delivery has one more possible future scenario that has its harbinger in the increasingly popular concierge medicine, in which patients pay the primary care physician a lump sum annually for the privilege of being preferentially cared for. It is therefore conceivable that a two-tier health-care system might emerge on a larger scale. Specifically, patients who do not want to wait in line and can afford it will take upon themselves some of the responsibility for defraying the increased cost of their preferential care. Such service-oriented class difference is not without precedent in an otherwise-egalitarian society (for example, airlines offer first and coach classes, but the pilot and safety are the same). It is essential, however, that physicians and health-care institutions recognize the imperative that preferentially serviced care must not become synonymous with better care or greater safety.

I am aware that my views on the current state of US health care are raising more questions than solutions regarding the existing inadequacies in maintaining the health of our nation. Whatever progress to that end is finally achieved, it will be a daunting task requiring extraordinary leadership to gradually change the attitudes of purpose of health-care consumers and providers who will be asked to partner in the recognition of the economic limitations of health-care delivery. This quest should be coupled with a meaningful reform of the medicolegal system. Clearly, each participant in this noble task of health-care delivery should and must be willing to relinquish some of the present self-oriented gestalt so that the United States can remain both healthy and fiscally sound.

THERE IS LIFE BEYOND WINNETKA

After I stepped down as the chief of neurosurgery in 2001, my associate Ted Eller assumed the mantle of leadership. His tenure was short, as he left our institution to pursue private practice in another Illinois town. Ted was succeeded by Hunt Batjer, the chair of the department of neurosurgery at Northwestern, and when he left to lead a renowned department in another state, by Julian Bailes who was recruited from the University of West Virginia where he chaired the department of neurosurgery. Ted, Hunt and Julian are superb surgeons and proven leaders. They recruited a number of talented and exceptionally skilled neurosurgeons to complement the needs for subspecialty areas in our department with whom I had the pleasure and privilege of collaborating in the waning years of my practice.

While all these leadership changes were happening, Anne and I decided to slowly start our descent in life by first downsizing from our elegant house in Winnetka to a duplex villa in a relatively new development in Northfield, some five miles west of our Winnetka home. Our children were off to colleges and later, after completing postgraduate studies, were eagerly carving out their own niches in life. We also purchased a lovely two-bedroom condo in Palm Desert. The sojourns to Palm Desert were always rejuvenating, as they helped rekindle our passion for each other, which might have suffered under the burden of my long working hours and the vagaries in my professional life. Besides the search for relatively predictable warm winter weather, another reason we chose a place in southwestern California was the abundance of hiking trails in the mountains surrounding the Coachella Valley. We hiked in the Indian Canyons and in the San Jacinto wilderness. On one occasion, we hiked up from Idyllwild to the summit of the San Jacinto peak at 11,800 feet. While in California, we also took up golf at the improbable age of sixty-plus, with no salutary results to make a story out of, other than being seduced by the game and meeting a lot of nice people along the way. The saying that golf builds character is only partially true; for sure, though, it does reveal character.

We also traveled a fair amount, not excessively or in search of an extreme adventure. We went to Europe usually once a year to visit siblings and to pay homage to the resting places of our ancestors. During these trips, we would also set aside time to enjoy our passion for hiking. In Switzerland, we trekked in stages along the Bear Trail in the Bernese Oberland, starting from the pastoral Grindelwald over the Kleine Scheidegg and the enchanted alpine resort of Wengen to Lauterbrunnen. From there, it was over Mürren and the Sefinenfurgge Pass to Golderli. We never made it over the Hohtürli, the highest hiking pass on the Bear Trail, although we tried to by hiking up from Kandersteg over Oeschinen Lake, where we stayed overnight. We took off at sunrise but turned around on my cowardly urging about six hours into the hike, with the pass in sight.

In Britain, we were attracted to the colors of spring in the Cotswolds, where Anne, always the passionate amateur archeologist, savored the visit to the earliest monuments of civilization in England. In Norway, on our way to a neurosurgery conference in Russia, we admired the majesty of the sheer cliffs of the Norwegian mountain ranges guarding the calm green waters of the fjords, which glittered like a mirror as my son and I rowed under the solstice's midnight sun. Getting to know the Scandinavian people, the fun-loving Danes in Copenhagen, the reticent and strict Norwegian highlanders, and the urbane Swedes in Stockholm was a distinct pleasure. On another occasion we savored the European atmosphere of Buenos Aires and the beauty of Patagonia as we crossed the Lake District into Chile. In Paris, the preferred landing port for our trips to Europe, we were attracted by the pulse of the city, reminiscent in its vibrancy of New York yet, in an artistic kind of way, very different from it. We liked walking along the glittering streets and avenues of the Right Bank and, after crossing the Seine, threading the narrow streets of the Left Bank, with a stop here or there for lunch, preferably at a lovely little spot on the Quai Voltaire or somewhere close to the Sorbonne. Exhausted and thirsty, we would call it a day after a Campari soda and dinner at a local bistro not far from our usual digs on Rue Astorg, wedged a stone's throw between the Élysée Palace and the Madeleine.

On a recent occasion, we traveled to Serbia to attend a commemoration honoring my father for his service to the old Kingdom of Yugoslavia. The commemoration, in conjunction with an exhibit, took place in the ornate, cavernous reception hall of the Serbian Parliament under the auspices of the president (speaker) of Parliament and the minister of education, two offices my father was privileged to occupy seventy-five years earlier. The commemoration, a direct result of the recent return to democracy in Serbia, was a posthumous vindication of my father's service to the nation, completing the circle of his life.

THE MIRACLE ON MAPLE COURT

Shortly before I retired from active practice, I took care of H, a retired Chicago surgeon and an old friend. H was passionate about his work, loving every day in the office and savoring every moment in the operating room. He is still a good-looking guy too, with kind of the Gay Twenties' good looks. His well-proportioned facial features are set on a usually slightly suntanned, barely freckled, and remarkably smooth face for an octogenarian. There is a sparkle in his eyes that is gently and fatherly mocking and approving at the same time. Oh yes, I forgot to mention his always well-groomed hair, which he parts on the side à la Jimmy Stewart. H is not exceptionally tall, though after years of standing at the operating table, he has developed a slight stoop, adding to his overall aristocratic appearance. What always drew my attention were his hands. Elegantly narrow yet crafty, his well-cared-for hands and fingers took part with obvious pleasure, but discreetly so, in the body language of a surgeon and connoisseur of life. H's patients adored him. They flocked to him not only because of his acumen as a physician or because of his surgical prowess but, I suspect, also because they considered him a friend to whom they could come for advice or simply to bare their souls. To be with H and to listen to his numerous stories and share in his humor meant coming away optimistic and uplifted.

On a balmy June day, H developed severe back pain that grew steadily worse. It almost doubled him over. Lost was his sunny countenance, replaced by the rigors of a man in agony. It took some time for the diagnosis of a spinal infection involving the lower thoracic and upper lumbar vertebrae to be made. The infected vertebrae were biopsied. Treatment with antibiotics, while temporarily effective in stemming the tide of infection, did not vanquish the disease or prevent infection-induced destruction of the vertebrae. After several weeks of conservative treatment, H developed an insidious onset of weakness in his legs; it was slow at first but became rapidly progressive over time. Finally, he could not stand, let alone walk. Additional imaging showed an accumulation of puss in his spine, compressing the spinal cord. There was no other choice but to proceed with surgery and relieve the pressure on the spinal cord. I was honored and humbled when H and his family asked me to proceed with surgery.

After a temporary improvement, H's infection caused him to deteriorate once again. This ushered in a period of days that turned into weeks and months of unimaginable pain unresponsive to all but the most potent narcotics. H remained bedridden and completely dependent on round-the-clock help, at first in the hospital and later at home in a hospice setting. This was also a period when despair and anguish overwhelmed his devoted wife and their children. They were desperate because their beloved husband and father was in constant pain, and they were anguished because of the burden of the decision they had to make whether to continue the battle for mere existence and a life without quality or to forsake the ethos of life and give up for the sake of humanity. The consensus was to transfer H to a regional spine center, where he would be evaluated for possible additional surgery. The thinking was that unless the infection was eradicated surgically, a formidable procedure that would require reconstruction and stabilization of the spine, H would have no chance for quality survival. Once there, he was deemed too feeble and fragile to proceed with surgery, no matter how minimally invasive it might be, and he was sent back to hospice care.

Yet the flickering flame of hope prevailed. Medical management with antibiotics and exceptionally superb around-the-clock care continued. Gradually, H began to respond, and his cognitive functions returned slowly but surely. When I visited him at his home, I noticed that his legs had regained some strength, though they were far from being functional. Interval imaging showed some improvement in the spinal infection, with less swelling and even some reformatting of the destroyed vertebrae. In time, though, the improvement stalled, and H's condition grew worse once again. The back pain again became steadily more bothersome, interfering with his rehabilitation. Repeat imaging showed that the healing process in and of itself had caused a new set of anatomic changes in the spine, resulting in spinal cord compression and a potentially threatening paralysis. After more soul searching, the family decided to have H reevaluated at the regional spine center. The consulting surgeon thought that the odds of the operation being successful, while still greatly stacked against my friend, were nevertheless better this time around, and he agreed to proceed. Therefore,

H underwent minimally invasive surgery to relieve the pressure and stabilize the spine. The initial postoperative course was rocky. H developed deep vein thrombosis and pulmonary embolism, requiring placement of a device called a filter into the major abdominal vein. For a while, H was barely responsive after surgery, but he gradually regained cognition as the pain medication was withdrawn. After nearly eighteen months of suffering and being relegated to hospice care, H gradually began to improve; he stood up and began to walk with the aid of a cane. The hospice bed was no more. His brilliant mind resurfaced. Oh yes, the twinkle in his eyes also returned. All along, his wife, a strong-willed woman with a remarkable moral compass, stood lovingly but with resolve by her man in her quest for compassion and hope while boldly facing reality and respecting dignity of life.

I chose to tell this story of success and social prominence turned into a nightmare and suffering because it is also a story of resilience, healing and healers, and, ultimately, hope and re-affirmation of life so richly deserved by this humble servant of life. It was a true miracle on Maple Court. Over the years, I have witnessed numerous similar stories of amazing and unexpected survival and recovery of patients in peril. Still, the question as to why some of these patients respond to treatment and some do not remains a mystery—a mystery that we can only answer in light of our intimacy with science and faith.

LESSONS LEARNED

Each and every patient who saw me in consultation over a period close to half a century, including those who required surgery, regardless of the outcome, has taught me a lesson in wisdom, humility, and humanity. Being honest and always taking the high road, not only as healers but also, just as importantly, with ourselves, is the only way to navigate the hurdles in life with our hearts at peace and our souls pure.

However, what practical lessons did I learn that have helped lessen the incidence of complications and, thus, increase the number of salubrious outcomes? Perhaps the fundamental lesson learned was that taking a careful history and performing a thorough neurological examination are the cornerstones for deriving the correct diagnosis, as they enable the neurosurgeon to initiate a cascade of appropriate decisions regarding the choice of diagnostic studies and treatment. Another important lesson was that it is far better to be prepared for all eventualities that might arise in the course of an operative procedure and in the postoperative period, to anticipate complications rather than to be blindsided by them. This requires experience, to be sure, but also a preoperative quiet time to reflect on the task at hand.

Hence, a busy practice geared toward increasing numbers of patients seen and operated on might prove detrimental in the long run if it leads to shortcuts in preoperative reflective assessment of a specific patient.

In the course of an operative procedure, it is preferable to be always vigilant under the motto "What can go wrong?" rather than to become emboldened by the smooth progress of an operation under the illusion that nothing can go wrong. The reason for this is that even a momentary lapse in concentration and guard can be an invitation for the disaster lurking around the corner to strike with vengeance. Attention to detail is another obvious prerequisite for a successful outcome of a neurosurgical procedure.

There is one more important lesson I learned through my own experience and from talking to and observing my colleagues at work. In the course of neurosurgical operations, neurosurgeons, especially novice neurosurgeons, would be well advised not to exceed their level of comfort. Neurosurgeons are well aware of the gut-wrenching feeling when they venture into an unchartered territory without the ability to bail out when in trouble. Hence, neurosurgeons should remain within their comfort zone, lest they crash down the path of a cascading series of complications. One can argue, though, that innovation and progress in neurosurgery have often been made by pioneering neurosurgeons who ventured into previously unchartered territory, broke the glass ceiling, succeeded in the process, and soared high. This does require a critical self-assessment of one's confidence and ability, which are rooted in the neurosurgeon's training and experience. A swashbuckling bravado venturing beyond the accepted norms without prior mentoring in a particular arena of neurosurgery and with no backing by extensive experience is bound to fail.

What about dealing with complications? Having the unfortunate opportunity to experience my own and witness the complications of other neurosurgeons, I have gotten the impression that neurosurgeons often tend to procrastinate in confirming the mishap and dealing with it accordingly in a timely fashion. Recognizing a complication early on and taking care of it with dispatch will more often than not save function and life.

Neurosurgeons are fortunate to be on the receiving end of ego-soothing expressions of gratitude by thankful patients on a daily basis, to a point where this praise can distort our self-image into a make-believe of glorified invincibility. It is important, therefore, for neurosurgeons to stay grounded by reminding ourselves of the despair brought on by our failures. With these thoughts in mind, I have embraced a number of attitudinal principles, some of which I will mention here.

Quiet rather than boisterous excellence is desirable. To that end, it is better to be self-effacing than boastful.

In this age of often less-than-critical digital self-promotion, the only true testimony of neurosurgeons' accomplishments is when our peers extol our virtues.

I have attended many quality-control conferences, also known as morbidity and mortality conferences, during which judgmental and especially technical mistakes were blamed on extraneous circumstances. A more self-oriented mea culpa attitude in this regard would probably be more conducive to avoiding repeating the same mistake; after all, experience is accrued and not declared.

In short, let us treat our patients with same attributes as we would like our family treated.

Perhaps the most enduring lesson is that neurosurgery is a specialty in evolution with a bright future. Besides the conventional indications discussed in these memoirs, the spectrum of neurosurgical interventions has recently widened to encompass a number of new functional disorders, including a host of movement disorders, obsessive-compulsive and other psychiatric disorders, and many more. Even more remarkable is the wide repertoire of modern surgical techniques designed to achieve minimal invasiveness, minimal pain, minimal downtime, maximal effectiveness and safety, and acceptable cost-effectiveness. The introduction of endovascular techniques in the treatment of vascular lesions of the brain and spinal cord, the increasing application of endoscopic techniques in accessing a variety of neurosurgical maladies, and the ever-greater reliance on focused high-energy radiation treatment are but a few technical advances that have contributed toward realizing the stated goals of modern neurosurgery. At the same time, the advances in neuroscience, especially in the molecular biology of brain tumors, have ushered in a host of alternative treatment paradigms.

IVAN CIRIC, MD

RETURNING HOME

About a year after I retired from practice, I began noticing some lack of agility in my dominant right hand. Shortly thereafter, my handwriting began to change, with letters getting ever smaller as I would continue to write. In time, Anne also noticed that I did not swing my right arm to the same degree as my left one while walking. It was only after I began noticing a lack of balance that I realized I had a neurological illness. Initially, I thought I had had a stroke, in view of my chronic hypertension. I saw a neurologist and had a series of imaging studies done, which ruled out a stroke and instead confirmed that I had developed a form of Parkinson's disease. The study that was most revealing was the DaTa radionuclide scan, which revealed decreased presynaptic dopaminergic uptake in the left putamen—a mouthful which simply means that my deep gray matter, the basal ganglia, is refusing to produce and store dopamine, the chemical responsible for the fluidity and smoothness of movements. Presently, I am on appropriate medication with salutary effectiveness.

I decided to return to my hometown one more time in the hope that being close to my roots would bring me the solace I am seeking at this stage in my life. Anne and the family came along for the trip. The idealized memory of my roots, firmly emblazoned in my heart, seemed to pale in the reality of today's Serbia, which is foreign and remote from the days of my youth, a country that seems to me in search of an identity in an interconnected world of political allegiances and economic blocks. Serbia's heart is in the East, and its raison d'être is in the West. There is palpable evidence of progress; both industrial development and small businesses seem to flourish. However, while the shiny testimonies of the twenty-first century, such as cyberspace and the availability of luxurious amenities, have deeply permeated the life in Serbia, the progress is not shared by all. As for health care, Serbia is fortunate to have a cadre of highly educated, talented, and experienced physicians and surgeons who perform admirably in a setting of less-than-glistening infrastructure.

The visit to my hometown of Sremski Karlovci evoked nostalgic memories of a homey town steeped in ancient traditions—memories that were in a way incongruous with the present-day pulse of the city. There are no more horse-drawn carriages, hand-driven presses at the time of the grape harvest, shepherds blowing their horns, or village crier. My old high school—surrounded by the familiar buildings and palaces in the town square, all restored to a gilded sheen—was admired by a group of foreign tourists bused in for the day. The motorized traffic was abundant enough for city fathers to establish a pedestrian-only zone. The Danube, still as stately as it used to be, is afflicted, I was told, with impurity. Even though it was the height of the summer, there were no bathers or swimmers. The ancient anglers' paddleboats of my youth, which used to bob up and down with the waves while chained to trees along the shore, have been replaced by a fleet of sleek motorboats moored in their berths in a makeshift marina. I admired the obvious progress while, I suppose foolishly so, longing for the bygone era. Back in Belgrade, which is a modern metropolis now, albeit scarred from the Allied bombers during the 1990s' war, I tried in vain to evoke the memories of my youth. The feverish feeling of anticipation of a glorious future that used to grip me while I prowled the streets of Belgrade and the cozy atmosphere of obscure little cafés that I used to frequent as a medical student, was no more. Surely, during our visit to Belgrade, we enjoyed the exquisiteness of Serbian cuisine and the Western accommodations, but the sense of belonging, sadly, was simply not there. After more than half a century of living and raising a family in this glorious land of ours, I was glad to be returning home. Still, I shall always remain proud of my Serbian ancestry and traditions and keep the memories of my youth close to my heart.

I believe I have reminisced enough. The only thing I would like to say before bowing out is that I am grateful for all the beneficence life has bestowed on me. I am grateful for the love and sacrifice of my parents. I am grateful to my dear Anne, my partner in life, for all the love she has given me, which has been much more so than I have or could ever give in return, and to our children and grandchildren for the joy of life. Above all, I am grateful for the privilege of having lived the bliss of a neurosurgeon's dream.

EPILOGUE

Neurosurgeon's Bliss

When faced with illness and despair,
For the frail woman, our heart cannot help but weep,
And yet our mind is resolute and science fair,
While our soul begins to soar and leap.
With the challenge all too tempting
And, yes, with humility of battles past,
We are determined to vanquish the miserable suffering
As we evoke Hippocrates and ask our God not to fail.
And here we are, lancet in hand,
Ready and energized yet not without fear,
For we are expected to wave the magic wand
As the waiting family and child pray and shed a tear.
With craftsman's tools, we enter the pantheon of humankind.
Our senses heightened and bright,
The masked, muffled chatter not to mind,
We labor under the microscope light.
As the gray curtain falls, the mystery of life is bared.
We admire our Maker's glowing art in awe and alone—
Here, careful, the memory's lair

And there the poet's Blarney Stone.
Two careful and gentle steps forward
we advance along the red river of life.
"Hold it—take one step backward,"
Whispers the honed instinct with a bit of strife.
Deeper and more perilous we venture
As we approach the devil incarnate.
Life or death can be this mother's future
Or, even worse, neither life nor death.
With disregard for all but the human,
Our heartbeat slower and our soul fuller,
We remember the teaching of our shaman,
And so finally, with steady hand, we conquer.
The retreat is full of hope and measured,
Since attention to detail, we were told,
Is where the ugly error finds its end,
So we can rejoice out there in the family fold.
"Alleluia!" sing the angels in our heart
As we bid adieu to science, craft, and art,
For it is the little one's hug and kiss
That is every neurosurgeon's heavenly bliss!

BIBLIOGRAPHY

Ammirati, M., N. Vick, Y. Liao, I. Ciric, and M. Mikhael. "Effect of the Extent of Surgical Resection on Survival and Quality of Life in Patients with Supratentorial Glioblastomas and Anaplastic Astrocytomas." *Neurosurgery* 21: 201-206, 1987.

Antin, Mary. *The Promised Land*. New York: Penguin, 2012.

Bradford, William. *Of Plymouth Plantation*. New York: Random House, 1981.

Ciric, I., A. Ragin, C. Baumgartner, and D. Pierce. "Complications of Transsphenoidal Surgery: Results of a National Survey, Review of Literature and Personal Experience." *Neurosurgery* 40: 225-237, 1997.

Ciric, I. and J.W. Cozzens. "Craniopharyngiomas—Transsphenoidal Method of Approach: For the Virtuoso Only?" *Clinical Neurosurgery* 27: 605-625, 1980.

Ciric, I., J. Zhao, S. Rosenblatt, R. Wiet, and B. O'Shaughnessy. "Suboccipital Retrosigmoid Approach for Removal of Vestibular Schwannomas with Facial Nerve Function and Hearing Preservation." *Neurosurgery* 56: 560-570, 2005.

Ciric. I, J. Zhao, H. Du, J.W. Findling, M. Molitch, S. Refetoff, R.W.Weiss. "Transsphenoidal Surgery for Cushing's

IVAN CIRIC, MD

Disease. Experience with 136 Patients." *Neurosurgery* 70: 70-80, 2012.

Ciric, I., S. Rosenblatt, and J. Zhao. "Transsphenoidal Microsurgery." *Neurosurgery* 51: 161-169, 2002.Ciric, I. and S. Rosenblatt. "Suprasellar Meningiomas." *Neurosurgery* 49: 1372-1377, 2001.

Ciric, I. "US Health Care: A Conundrum and a Challenge." *World Neurosurgery* 80: 691-698, 2013.

Ciric, I. *Fehldiagnosen bei Grosshirngeschwuelsten mit Stauungspapille.* Inaugural Dissertation. Cologne: Gouder u Hansen, 1964.

Cushing, Harvey. *Consecratio Medici.* Boston: Little, Brown, and Co., 1928.

Jelsma, R. and P.C. Bucy. "The Treatment of Glioblastoma Multiforme of the Brain." *Journal of Neurosurgery* 27: 388-400, 1967.

Proust, Marcel. *In Search of Lost Time, Swann's Way.* New York: Modern Library, 1992.

Stone, J., G. Meglio, and E. Laws. *Development of Pituitary Surgery: The Chicago Contributions.* Chicago: Journal of the American College of Surgeons, 2005.

ABOUT THE AUTHOR

Ivan Ciric, MD, is Emeritus Professor of Neurosurgery at Northwestern University Feinberg School of Medicine. He earned the doctor of medicine degree from the University of Belgrade in 1958 and from the University of Cologne in 1964. Ciric retired from active practice in 2011. He and his wife, Anne, live in Northfield, Illinois.

60433770R00158

Made in the USA
Lexington, KY
07 February 2017